The Right Hand According To Tatum

A Guide To Tatum's
Improvisational Techniques
Plus 10 Transcribed Piano Solos

by Riccardo Scivales

Copyright ©1998 Ekay Music, Inc.

Ekay Music, Inc., 2 Depot Plaza, Bedford Hills, New York 10507
Call Toll Free 1-800-527-6300
USA: musicbooksnow.com
Europe: goodmusic.co.uk

To my father

Acknowledgments

I would like to thank the Publisher, Edward J. Shanaphy (to whom I owe the idea to realize this book) and Stuart Isacoff. Also, I wish to express my gratitude to the following people who provided material and support in various ways: Giuliano Bianco, Stefano Biosa, Romolo Calciati, Elena Camerin, Giorgio Cuscito, Franco Fayenz, Mauro Fiorin and Giuliano Bontempelli of Telex, Marco Fumo, Nicola Gabrielli, Dick Hyman, Gunnar A. Jacobsen, Vasco Magnolato, Antonio Marotta, Louis Mazetier, Anna Maria and Adriano Mazzoletti, Alessandro Monti, Giovanni Morelli and Angelo Zaniol of the University of Venezia, Luigi Onori, Andrea Piovan, Marcello Piras, Becca Pulliam, Roberto Rusconi, Johnny Simmen, and Stefano Zenni. A most affectionate thank you goes to Enrica and to sweet newborn baby Giulia.

Contents

Preface

Among his outstanding musical skills, Art Tatum (1909-1956) had an amazing right hand, the strongest of his time and probably the strongest in the whole history of jazz piano. He was capable of sustaining dazzling, uninterrupted sixteenth-note motion throughout an entire chorus. He loved to play lightning-fast right hand licks up and down several octaves of the keyboard.

These runs and licks were not as repetitive as some jazz critics have claimed (to the indignation of the great majority of jazzmen, who always praised Tatum). On the contrary, Tatum used his right hand devices in a very imaginative and versatile way, and it is worth exploring these in order to incorporate them in our own playing. In the following pages, we will take a closer look at the master's right hand techniques, analyzing them and finding useful adaptations for those of us who are mere mortals.

"Tatum! You can't imitatum!" once wrote Barry Ulanov: this is an undeniable fact in the light of Tatum's unparalleled piano mastery (nor should any musician engage in the slavish imitation of another musician's style). This notwithstanding, if we cannot play the whole piano as Tatum did, we can at least try to better understand his right hand approach, and to enjoy the inspiration it provides.

This book is structured in two sections. Part One deals with the most recurrent of Tatum's right hand runs, licks, and phrases, which have been grouped together according to their general characteristics and functions. It is recommended that you transpose and practice these right hand devices in all the applicable keys, and elaborate on them in your own style. Part Two includes ten piano solos transcribed from Tatum recordings in piano solo, trio, and various groups settings. Each piano solo is preceded by an introductory note which further analyzes Tatum's style and right hand concepts. Needless to say, in order to have a fuller comprehension of the printed music it will be of invaluable help to listen to these recordings. Especially to Tatum neophytes, this will prove to be a most amazing musical experience.

Part One

Tatum's Right Hand Techniques

Introducing Some Of Tatum's
Right Hand Figures

This introductory chapter is a survey of some of Tatum's distinctive right hand runs, and their possible adaptations and applications. Let's start with a quite simple figure. This is a basic example of a right hand run often played by Tatum on the D7 chord (this figure can also be played in different rhythms; Tatum often used it in the modified form also shown):

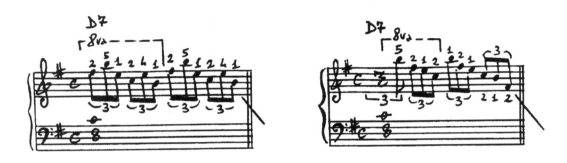

Notice that this is a six-note figure, repeated in different octaves. It is made up of two groups of notes, i.e. F#-B-E and C-E-B, played with the repeated fingerings 2-5-1/2-4-1, and so on. This fingering makes the run very easy and fun to play, as shown below:

Now let's analyse the pattern of Fig. 1. It is made up of the 2nd, 3rd, 6th, and 7th degrees of the D7 (Mixolydian) scale, played in the order shown below:

Following this pattern and keeping the same 2-5-1/2-4-1 repeated finger-ing, we can transpose the first figure to various other dominant seventh chords, such as Eb7, G7, or C7. Here is an example on the F7 chord:

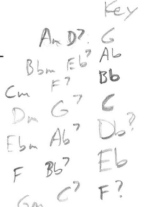

Also notice that this figure can be used in a ii7 / V7 / I progression in G Major (remember to transpose this application to other keys):

However, the basic pattern fits many other chords as well—such as Cm7, Am6/9, F#m7/b5, B7, and Em9:

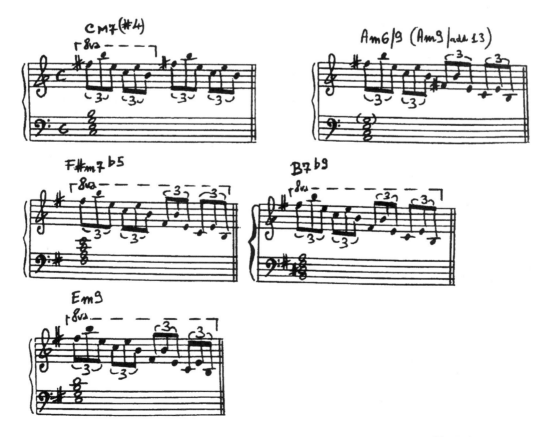

The following example shows a rhythmic adaptation of our initial figure, for use in a ii7 / V7 / I progression in E minor (it could be used, for instance, in measures 5-8 and 13-16 of "Autumn Leaves"). Try to make up your own adaptations as you go along.

Let's not stop there. Tatum's run turns out to be even more flexible. By turning all the C's into C#'s, in fact, it will fit an A7/13 chord as well as a ii7 / V7 / I in D Major (be sure to transpose this device to other keys as well):

(In the last example, the final bar introduces a kind of ascending "broken" arpeggio often used by Tatum to conclude his phrases.)

Notice how many possible applications we can get starting from a simple six-note figure actually made of just four tones!

Now let's move on to another distinctive and more demanding Tatum run, taken from the end of the interlude of his trio recording of "Body And Soul," issued on Black Lion BLP 30203:

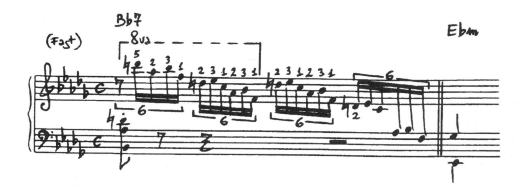

This figure is a right hand run played on the Bb7 chord. Starting from its second note, we can see that it is another six-note descending run repeating in different octaves. It is made up of two groups of notes (Ab-Bb-F and D-Eb-C) played with the repeated 2-3-1 fingering, which makes this figure easy and fun to play. Notice how the right hand "runs" on the keyboard without effort:

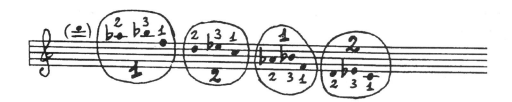

Analyzing its pattern, we can see that it uses the 7th, 8th, 5th, 3rd, 4th, and 2nd degrees of the Bb7 (Mixolydian) scale:

Following this pattern and keeping the same 2-3-1 repeated fingering, the run can be transposed and played on other dominant seventh chords, such as C7, Db7, D7, Eb7, F7, G7, Ab7, and A7. I suggest you practice them until you can instantly associate the run with its chord.

Here is an example on the C7 chord:

Again, notice how it fits a ii7 / V7 / I in Eb Major too (the run is here played in sixteenth notes):

Yet, without changing any note, you can adapt this run to the Cm7 chord as well as to a Dm7b5 G7 / Cm7 cadence:

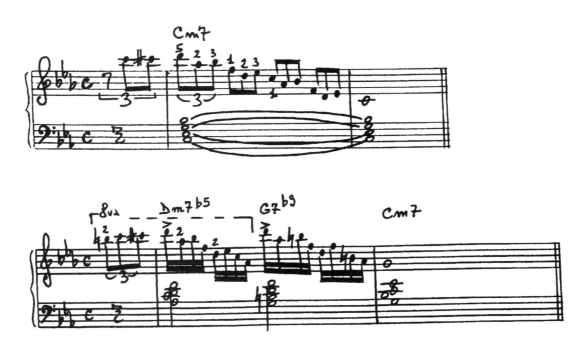

The Right Hand According To Tatum

By turning all the D's of this figure into Db's, we get a run that fits the ii7 / V7 / I cadence in both Db and Ab Major:

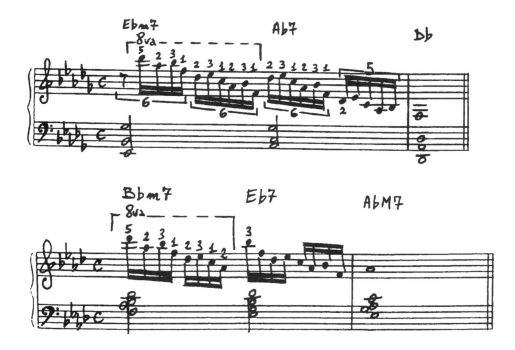

Now let's explore a new pattern for another brilliant descending run often played by Tatum on the Bb7 chord (various examples are found in collections of piano solos and transcriptions listed at the end of this book):

This figure is made up of the 6th, 7th, 5th, 3rd, 4th, and 2nd degrees of the Bb7 (Mixolydian) scale. Again, it is a six-note run set apart in two groups of three notes each, played with the repeated fingering 2-3-1:

By keeping the same 2-3-1 fingering on all of these runs, they can be played with different rhythms, and start from different pitches and parts of the measure. Their applications are virtually countless. See for instance the examples below and practice them:

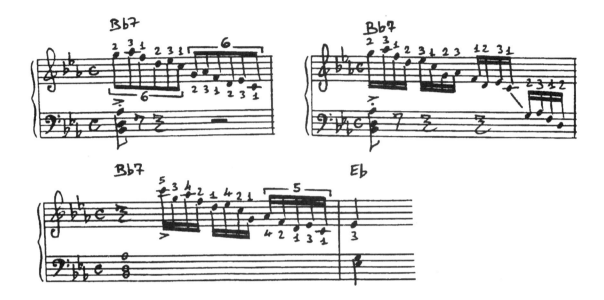

Tatum also used a variant of this pattern by adding a perfect fourth above the first note of each triplet. Notice how effective this is, and how easily it falls under the hand:

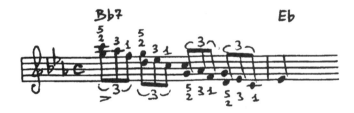

Keeping the same 2-3-1 repeated fingering, the run can be easily transposed and played on the following dominant seventh chords:

The Right Hand According To Tatum

It is easy to see that all the runs just shown fit the ii7 / V7 / I cadence (for instance, the run on the F7 chord can be played on a Cm7 / F7 / Bb cadence as well). But this run on the F7 chord also works for an Am7b5 / D7 / Gm cadence. The general rule on that is: all these runs can be played for a ii7 / V7 / I progression, where the "I" chord is a whole-step above the dominant seventh chord on which the run is built. Here is the example in G minor (the last two bars also feature the previously found ascending "broken" arpeggio):

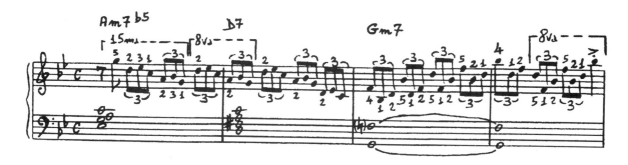

In order to avoid duplicating Tatum too exactly, you can practice playing short phrases of your own and resolving them with Tatum's licks. See for instance the example below, still on a ii7 / V7 / I in G minor (you can think of the beginning of the bridge of "Alone Together," as well as countless other familiar songs):

Tatum used blues devices too. Here is a repeated blues lick he played beginning the second chorus of "Lady Be Good," recorded September 16, 1941 (issued on Onyx 205). Notice how this figure easily fits a turnaround in G Major:

The tone pattern of this figure, shown in G, is easily transposed to the keys of C, D, F, and Bb Major. Here is an example in C Major:

As a simple application of this figure, try repeating it over and over on the complete 12-bar blues changes. In the last two measures, notice the resolution with a Tatumesque right hand "broken" arpeggio, which implies a C13/#11 chord:

Another bluesy lick, found in the opening of the 4th chorus of the January 21, 1946 V-Disc piano solo recording of "9.20 Special" (reissued on Black Lion BLCD760114), is shown below. Tatum played the following repeated figure on a G Major chord:

The pattern is easily recognizable and usable in many situations (just remember that it starts on the 5th of the chord). Here are some transposed examples (in the figures on C, F, and Bb, keep the same fingering):

It is easy to see that the figure used above for the G Major chord also fits a ii7 / V7 / I progression in G Major (here that figure is resolved by a descending pentatonic run):

as well as in a complete turnaround in G Major:

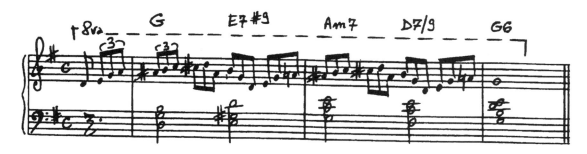

As we will see in more detail later in this book, Tatum's runs can be mixed together to form longer units. For instance, the following example (on the chord changes of "Autumn Leaves") begins with the last figure we examined, and is resolved by the rhythmic adaptation of the run shown earlier, while bar 4 features a descending pentatonic, and bar 3 a "climbing" run (for more on these last two devices, see the next chapters in this book):

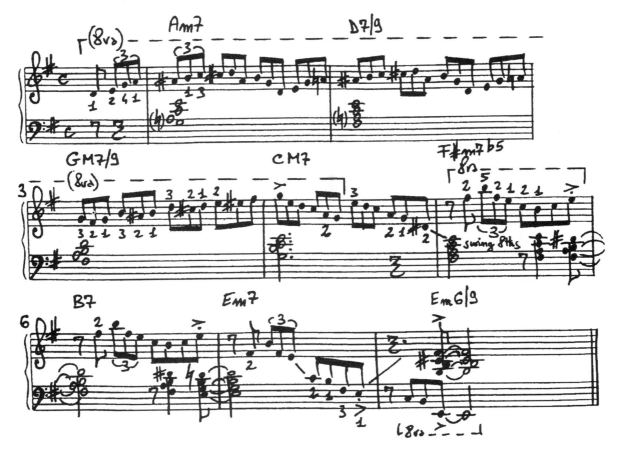

In the next example (on a 12-bar blues chorus in G), our G Major figure has been linked with other distinctive Tatum runs which you will find discussed later in this book):

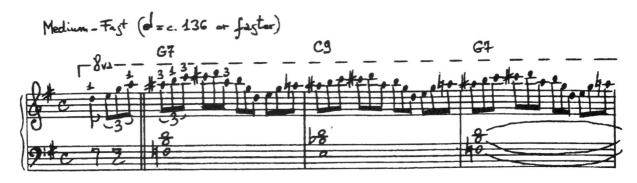

On many occasions, Tatum loved to insert a dissonant, short lick, illustrated by the following two examples (taken, respectively, from the transcriptions of "Esquire Bounce" and "Knockin' Myself Out" in this book):

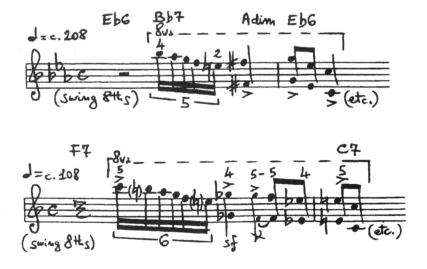

A longer variant to these is the sparkling run on a turnaround in Eb Major, played by Tatum in the last two bars of the second chorus of his 1944 great live recording of "Ain't Misbehavin'" (on Black Lion BLP 30203). Bass notes here have been added for harmonic reference (Tatum plays the changes indicated by the chord symbols):

You can practice transposing this run for use in turnarounds in the keys of C, F, G, and Bb Major.

A different resolution to the longer variant is found in bars 9-10 of the Tatum chorus in the 1945 group recording of "Royal Garden Blues" (on Joker SM 3117):

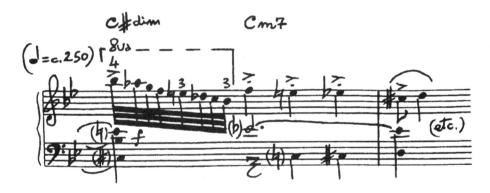

An even more sparkling right hand run (from bars 7-8 of the third chorus of the above-mentioned recording of "Ain't Misbehavin'") is played on a turnaround in Eb Major. Tatum made frequent use of this run, which is clearly based on the keyboard layout. The run is made possible by the thumb sliding from black keys to white keys in the third and fourth note of each group of sixteenths. The fingering for this lick is always 5-4-1-1. Notice the resolution too:

The Right Hand According To Tatum

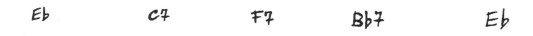

As we can see, the pattern for the lick in four-note groups shown above is the following: 1) starting note; 2) the note a half-step (or a whole-step) below the starting note; 3) the note one octave below the second note; 4) the note a half step below the third note; then a new starting note one octave above the fourth note, etc. The second and the third note of each group are always on black keys:

Tatum made extensive use of this lick, on many different types of changes, and starting from different pitches. He was able to run it over the keyboard for more than three bars—as it occurs in the closing of the second chorus of the 1941 "Lady Be Good" on Onyx 205. Another application, starting on the upbeat, is found in the transcription of his solo on "Esquire Bounce" in this book. For practicing this run, you could try the following drill, starting slowly and then gradually increasing the speed until you are playing as fast as you can:

We can try to combine Tatum's distinctive runs into longer units than he himself did. Here is a simple application on the chord changes of the bridge of "I Got Rhythm," using the runs previously discussed. In the third and fourth bar another Tatum run—to be discussed later—has been used:

Many other Tatum runs will be discussed in the following chapters of this book. For now, here is an example of his improvisatory phrasing on a I6 / IIIb7 / II7 / V7 / I turnaround in Eb Major (still from the above-mentioned 1944 recording of "Ain't Misbehavin'," bars 9-10 of the third chorus). Notice the alternation of arpeggios and descending chromatic passages which is so distinctive of his style:

For an example of Tatum's distinctive elongated endings, we can turn to the following measures transcribed form the 1950 piano solo recording of "I'm Gonna Sit Right Down and Write Myself a Letter." After the customary ii7 / V7 / I cadence, in fact, Tatum plays a series of secondary dominant seventh chords leading to the I chord again (in the third and fourth bars, the transcription of the left hand part is an approximation of what Tatum actually plays—in any case, the chord changes are correct):

Descending Pentatonic Runs

The figure below is a basic example of one of the most recurrent, showy, and well-known Tatum licks, i.e. a descending run built on the tones of the pentatonic "major" scale (in its ascending form, this scale is made of the 1st, 2nd, 3rd, 5th, and 6th degrees of the major scale). Tatum played this kind of run either on major chords or on dominant seventh chords, as well as on turnarounds, etc. Notice the characteristic approaching triplet too:

From many sources we also know that Tatum mostly fingered his pentatonic runs (as well as other runs) with only his first three fingers. On this matter, it is interesting to report the personal recollections of Billy Taylor and Jess Stacy—two jazz pianists who knew Tatum well and observed his style first-hand. In his book Jazz Piano—A Jazz History (Dubuque, Iowa: Wm C.

Brown Company), Taylor—who also was a Tatum friend and protégé—has remembered the "impromptu" lessons Tatum often gave to many aspiring pianists at the Hollywood Bar at 133rd and 7th Avenue in New York: "Tatum" frequently showed many of us the proper fingering for some of the pentatonic runs he was so fond of."

While remembering Art Tatum in an interview reported in Benny Goodman and the Swing Era by James Lincoln Collier (New York: Oxford University Press), Jess Stacy said that "Tatum had a way to play scales with his thumb and first two fingers, instead of all five as customary, although he was adept at the standard method, too; the point was that by using only the stronger digits he could play a more even run. They called it 'the bowling ball technique,' because only the thumb and first two fingers are used to grasp a bowling ball."

Tatum used these pentatonic runs on many different chords, and in various performance situations. He played them with different rhythmic groupings and used different starting notes, at times covering the full keyboard range. Following are some examples—also taken from Tatum's actual recordings and/or arrangements—you can practice and transpose (notice the chromatic resolution of this run):

(Notice how this Eb pentatonic run is resolved by a few descending chromatic notes, then by a two-octave skip from middle C to the low Bb played by the left hand):

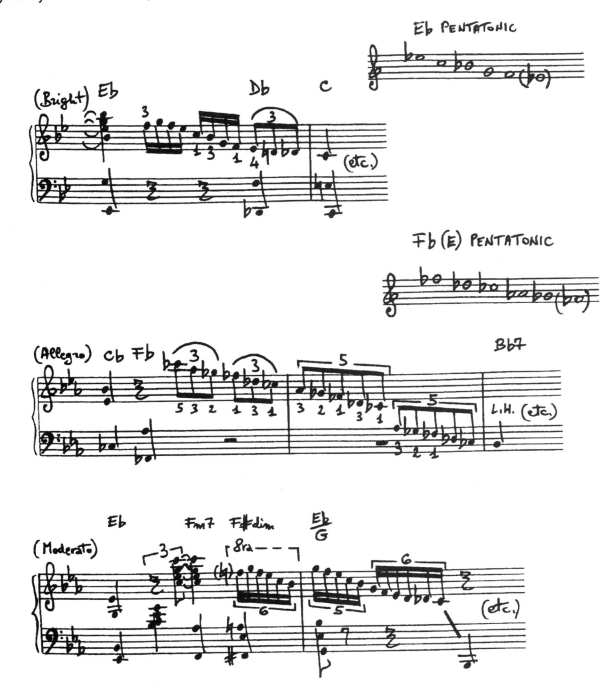

The Right Hand According To Tatum

All the pentatonic runs built on a I chord fit V7 / I and ii7 / V7 / I cadences. See the following two examples in F Major:

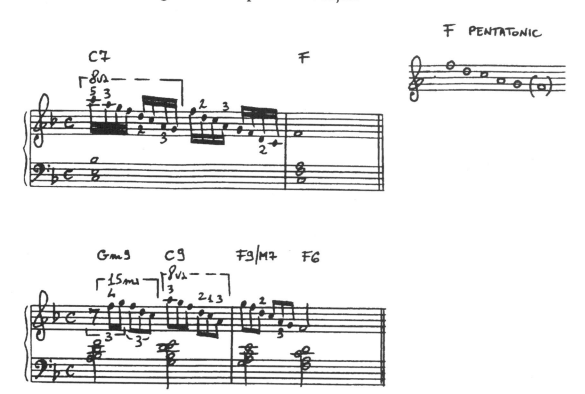

These pentatonic runs can be used in a complete I / vi7 / ii7 / V7 / I turn-around too:

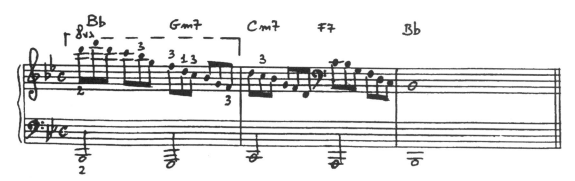

Here is another possible application on a well-known progression used in "I Got Rhythm" and many other tunes:

When using this run in a turnaround, you can begin with a descending pentatonic run and then add chromatic figures. See for instance the following excerpt from bars 7-8 of the second chorus of Tatum's 1944 solo recording of "Ain't Misbehavin'" (on Black Lion):

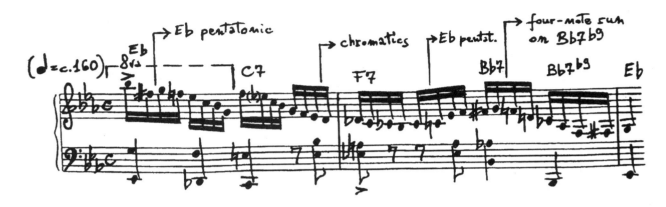

One of Tatum's most spectacular applications of a descending pentatonic run comes from the last chorus of his 1944 trio recording of "Moonglow" (transcribed in this book). Notice how this run fills the entire range of the keyboard (also take note of the contour of the opening figure):

The master managed to find other ways to apply this run, through harmonic innovation. Here is an excerpt from the famous introduction to "Begin The Beguine," recorded many times throughout his career. You can see this as a bitonal episode: the right hand plays a descending Eb pentatonic major run over an ostinato bass which outlines the D Major home key:

Here is another example of how Tatum joined members of the descending pentatonic run by means of descending connective chromatic notes. The following excerpt is from bars 7-8 of "Esquire Bounce" transcribed in this book (notice the resolution):

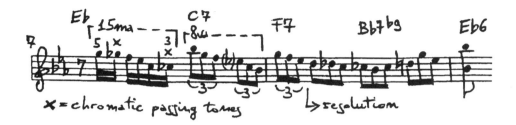

Here is another example in C Major:

Ascending chromatic passages can be used to connect two different descending pentatonic runs. That's what Tatum does in the following excerpt from bars 4-6 of the chorus in the 1945 group recording of "Royal Garden Blues" (on Joker SM 3117). A Bb pentatonic run (bar 4) and an Eb pentatonic run (bar 5) are linked together by a short ascending chromatic scale, thus forming a longer phrase (further resolved in bar 6 with descending chromaticism):

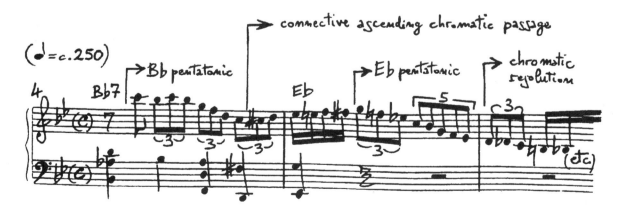

By using chromatic connective passages (and perhaps a few skips), you can link a pentatonic run with any other of Tatum's runs, thus forming longer and more complex phrases. Here is an example from "Ain't Misbehavin'," bars 67-68:

Another of Tatum's descending runs is also based on the tones of the pentatonic major scale. This one was used by Thomas "Fats" Waller (a strong and much-acknowledged influence on Tatum himself). The example below uses an Ab pentatonic scale and is taken from Tatum's arrangement of "Runnin' Wild." Notice the repeated fingering:

This kind of run falls easily under the hands when played on certain chords, including Db, Ab, Eb, and Bb. You can try transposing it to other major chords as well. It also fits the relative minor chords (for instance, the Ab run works for Fm too). Here is an application on a ii7 / V7 / I in Eb, resolved by another Tatum four-note run to be discussed later in this book:

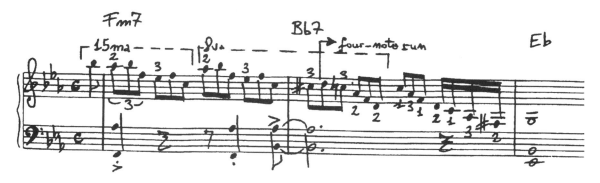

Tatum used a special device to elongate his descending pentatonic runs, to sustain them over longer groups of bars. In addition to inserting descending chromatic connective tones, he also inserted some ascending skips (usually fourths, fifths, or sixths), followed by a descending skip landing a whole-step or a half-step below any of the tones of the pentatonic run he was using. In this way, he was able to "gain" some ground, and was then ready to play another portion of the descending pentatonic run. Here are two simple examples:

Here is a more extended example-exercise based on this "gaining keys" device, applied to common chord changes in Bb Major. In the second and third bar, notice the insertion of a few descending chromatic connecting tones. Try to adapt this exercise to other pentatonic runs:

Descending "Five-Note Runs"
On Dominant Seventh Chords

On dominant seventh chords, Tatum often used another kind of descending pentatonic run: a five-note run built on the tones of a ninth chord. Here is a basic example (again, notice the fingering):

These five-note runs were usually preceded by some "approaching" tones, like those shown below (transpose these figures to other chords, such as Db7, D7, E7, A7, and Bb7, adjusting the fingering when necessary):

Like the runs discussed in the previous chapter, these can start from any note and at any point within the bar. They also fit ii7 / V7 / I cadences. Here are some examples of this (further examples are found in the transcribed solos in this book). Notice again the emphasis on the use of the first three fingers:

The following are two more extended examples, also linking Tatum's five-note runs to other phrases within common chord progressions, such as the Blues and the I / I#dim / ii7 / V7 / I sequence (try to make up some of your own):

The Right Hand According To Tatum

These five-note runs are often resolved by descending chromatic tones, as in the following example from bars 3-4 of the first chorus of the 1945 trio recording of "Sweet Georgia Brown" (on Joker SM 3117):

Short descending chromatic passages are also used to connect some tones of a five-note run. See for instance bars 21-24 from the first chorus of the above-mentioned "Sweet Georgia Brown" (notice the ascending skips too):

Here is another example, applied to an F7 five-note run on a ii7 / V7 / I progression in Bb Major:

When thinking about these kinds of patterns, keep in mind the "gaining keys" device we discussed at the end of the previous chapter. Here are two examples, still applied to the F7 descending five-note run (practice others, too):

It's a good idea to find creative ways to practice the aforementioned devices. Here is a possible example started by a simple phrase on the Cm7 chord and resolved by a F7 five-note run in which both the "gaining keys" trick and connecting chromatic tones have both been used:

Tatum's descending runs were inspiring to other jazz pianists of his time, such as the great—and rather overlooked—Herman Chittison. Here is a Chittison run on a C7b9 chord, from his 1941 solo recording of "The Man I Love" (issued on Meritt 20 and transcribed in the magazine *Piano Today*, May/June 1996). Easily transposable to chords like F7b9, G7b9, and Bb7b9, this run is a five-note figure repeated over the octaves:

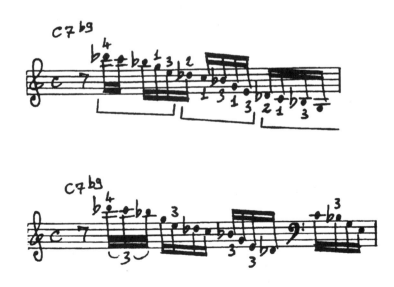

Descending "Four-Note Runs" On Dominant Seventh Chords

A type of descending run often used by Tatum on dominant seventh chords is made up of just four notes repeated over and over. It is used in the following excerpt taken from an improvisation on "Moonglow." In this figure, also notice the approaching triplet:

The run is built on the tones (excluding the root) of the Bb9 chord, i.e. the 2nd, 3rd, 5th, and 7th degrees of the Bb7 (Mixolydian) scale:

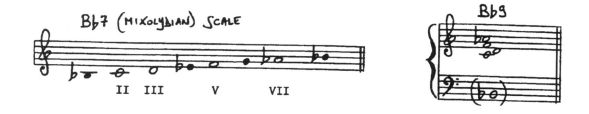

Of course, this kind of run fits ii7 / V7 / I cadences as well. Here is an example in Eb (also notice the different approaching tones, rhythmic articulation, and resolution):

This figure can be transposed to fit all the dominant seventh chords, with varied rhythmic articulations, starting points, approaching notes, and resolutions. The first example is a very simple one and also comes from "Moonglow":

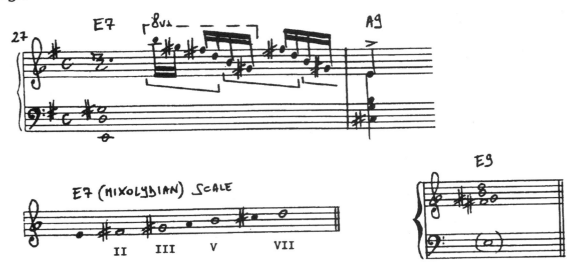

Here is a more articulated example, taken from bar 4 of the transcription of "Indiana" in this book. Notice the approaching tones and the resolution on the third to the next chord:

Often, the four-note descending run is approached and resolved by means of chromatic notes, as in the following excerpt from bar 8 of "Indiana":

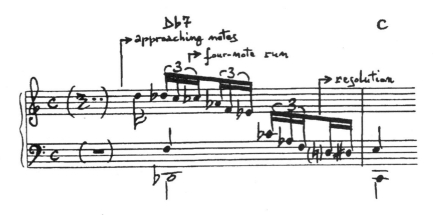

A similar example comes from the second chorus of "Sugar Foot Stomp" (group recording made in 1945):

Any four-note run can also be adapted to a dominant seventh chord with a flatted ninth, as Tatum did in bars 82-83 of the transcription of "After You've Gone":

Another very recurrent variant of these four-note runs employs the 6th degree of the Mixolydian scale in place of the 5th degree. Tatum used this new figure mostly on Am7 and the D7 chords. See the following excerpt from bar 37 of "Moonglow" (notice the approaching triplet):

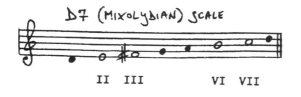

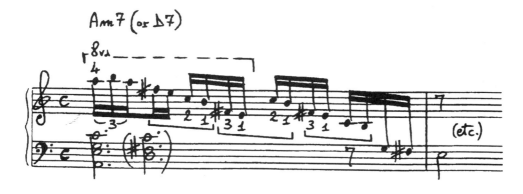

Also notice how this same figure fits a ii7 / V7 / i in E minor.

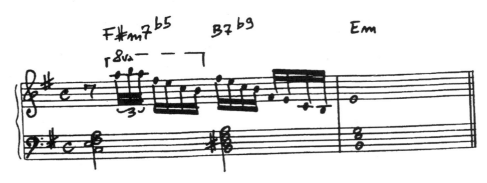

Tatum seemed to be very fond of the figure shown above, and used it extensively.

The descending four-note runs on dominant seventh chords are often found linked with other distinctive patterns. In the following example, see how Tatum started the 3rd chorus of his 1945 group recording of "Sugar Foot Stomp" (a blues piece), playing first a "climbing" run and then the four-note run previously shown:

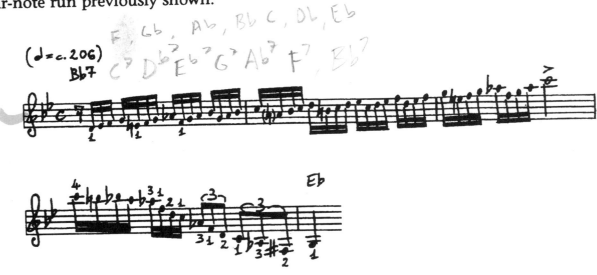

Try starting a phrase of your own and then resolve it with a Tatum four-note run. Here is a possible example on a ii7 / IIb7 / V progression in C Major:

Practice playing these Tatum four-note runs in different musical situations, trying your own solutions as well.

"Climbing" Runs

As a rival attraction to his distinctive descending runs, Tatum had a wide repertory of ascending runs which seemed to "climb" furiously up on the keyboard (some of these "climbing" runs are also found in the Breaks and Classical Devices chapters in this book). Following is a simple "climbing" run he played in his August 22, 1934 piano solo recording of "Cocktails For Two." The pattern of this run is very easy to see; it is made of repeated groups of six sixteenths, falling across the bar lines:

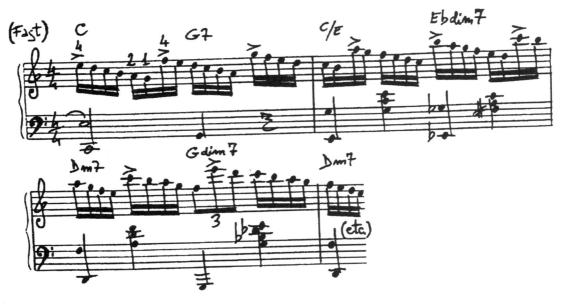

Here is just one of the many possible applications on a well-known progression in C Major:

The Right Hand According To Tatum

The "climbing" six-note figure can also have a different shape, as in the following example on a ii7 / V7 / I progression in Bb (also see examples in the "Breaks" chapter):

"Climbing" runs can be made of repeated groupings of just four notes, played either on the beats or across the beats. See the following three excerpts from the transcriptions of "Esquire Bounce," "Indiana," and "Moonglow":

For another example, here is a beautiful "climbing" run on an A7 chord. Tatum played this in bars 19-20 of the first chorus of his December 20, 1952 great recording of "Indiana" (on Capitol CDP 7 928672, Vols. 1 & 2):

The run shown above can be easily transposed to other chords, and adapted to ii7 / V7 / I cadences, where the I chord is a whole step below the dominant seventh chord on which the run is built. That is:

In the aforementioned "Indiana," as well as in various other recordings, Tatum used very simple "climbing" runs of this kind, with little variants:

This is a flashy and very adventurous "climbing" run made of ascending thirds on the Ab7 chord. Tatum played it on his 1933 recording of "Tiger Rag":

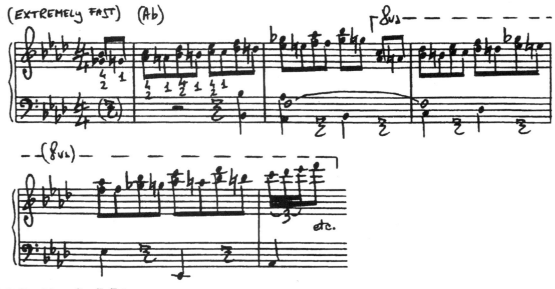

This figure is built on consecutive thirds taken from the Ab7 (Mixolydian) scale—here shown in whole notes—connected by chromatically ascending passing tones:

Due to its particular configuration on the piano keyboard, this pattern seems difficult to transpose and play at a proper speed on other dominant seventh chords. However, without transposing the figure shown above, you could utilize it on a Db Maj7 chord.

Just play all the "vertical" thirds of the previous figure as "horizontal" thirds and you will have another very effective—but much easier—"climbing" run. It is found in the ending of the Tatum's arrangement of "Runnin' Wild," where this run is sustained throughout six full measures! Notice the (suggested) repeated fingering 2-4-1:

Again, this "climbing" run is built on the tones of the Ab7 (Mixolydian) scale—here shown in whole notes. Notice that all the passing tones are chromatically ascending, except the C's and the F's. Here is the pattern:

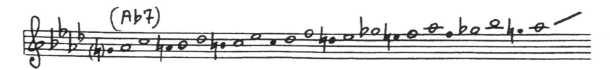

The "climbing" run above can be transposed to various dominant seventh chords. See the following example on the C7 chord, which requires a different fingering:

When played at the proper (i.e. fast) speed, this run can be very effective and fit a variety of musical situations. Here is a possible adaptation of the C7 run to a ii7 / V7 / I in F Major. Notice the choice of the starting note:

Tatum also adapted this run to major (i.e., not dominant seventh) chords. See for instance the following excerpt from his December 1935 oustanding recording of "Happy Feet," 4th chorus, bars 13-14 (reissued on Music & Arts CD 673). Notice the fingering that keeps the thumb on the white keys:

Here is the pattern transposed in C Major (also beginning on the "B" note), with adjusted fingering:

Of course, this kind of run can be played on a ii7 / V7 / I progression too:

and can be mixed with other Tatum runs so to create longer lines:

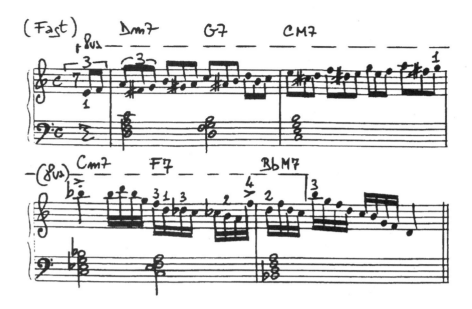

Finally, remember that you can start playing this run beginning from any of its first three notes, using different starting points in the measure, as well as with rhythms other than the triplets. See, for instance, the following four examples and try your own applications too:

A similar "climbing" run is found in Tatum's own composition "Amethyst," originally published in 1939 in England:

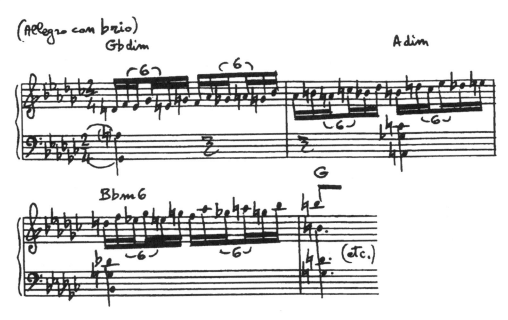

The pattern here is an ascending series of skips of minor thirds, played in triplets and using all the notes of the chromatic scale. This figure can be applied to the circle of fifths (notice that the figure here starts on the tonic of the first chord, and is resolved with Tatum's distinctive descending figure):

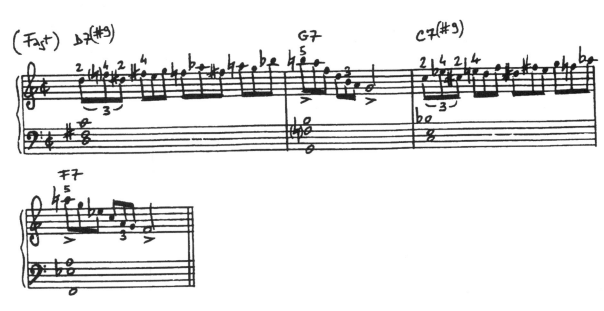

This pattern works well if we begin it on the 5th of the minor seventh chord in a ii7 / V7 / I cadence. Here is an application on the well-known ii7 / V7 / I / IV chord change, resolved by a typically Tatumesque ascending arpeggio (this example can be transposed to all keys):

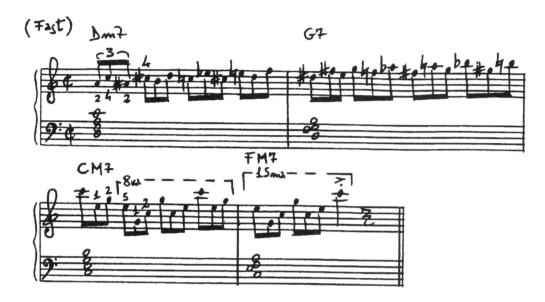

Another possible application is to begin on the 3rd of the I chord in the well-known I / I#dim / ii7 / V7 chord change. Here is an example in C Major (transpose it to other keys too):

Next is a "climbing" run taken from Tatum's May 7, 1941 recording of "Fine and Dandy," issued on Onyx 205. The pattern of this complex, dissonant run can be understood when placed in context of the F6 chord tones (shown in circlets) and can be used in various situations, for instance as an ascending run to end a piece. The fingering is our suggestion:

In his famous 1933 recording of "Tiger Rag," Tatum articulated this run in a different manner on I / V7 / I / V7 in F Major:

Another rhythmic variant used by Tatum is the following taken from the transcription of his 1933 version of "Tea for Two":

Now let's see some possible applications of the run. It can fit a ii7 / V7 / I in F Major:

It can also be played on a ii7 / V7 / I in C Major (notice that this "climbing" run has been resolved here with a descending pentatonic run):

In order to have a more rhythmic phrase, you might choose to play just the first fragment of this run, and then repeat that fragment on various octaves,

or transposed to other chords, such as C, Eb, G, and Bb.

In bars 9-12 of "I Got Rhythm" and 45-52 of "After You've Gone" (both transcribed in this book), you will notice long right hand phrases which start with a "climbing" run on the Bb chord. Notice that the "climbing" run starts on different rhythmic points, and that the chord changes as well as their resolutions are different:

The pattern of the above-mentioned "climbing" run is easy to see. It is made of some diatonic tones of the Bb Major scale (shown in circlets), each followed by two descending chromatic tones. The diatonic tones (shown below in full notes) are the 3rd, 5th, 6th, 7th, 9th, and 10th degrees of the Bb Major scale. The run also starts with an arpeggio on the Major 6th chord. Here is the pattern, transposed to C Major:

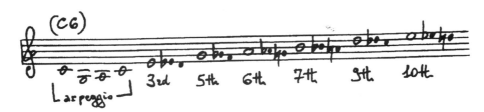

The Right Hand According To Tatum

A variant is the "climbing" run created by Tatum in his improvisation on "Knockin' Myself Out." Notice the differences in choice of diatonic tones, rhythm, and starting notes:

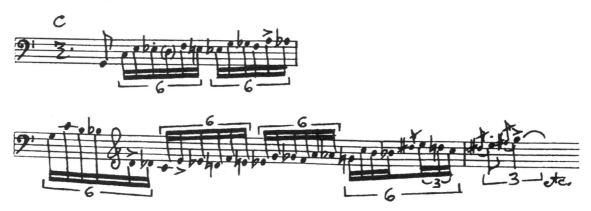

All in all, it seems that Tatum used all of these "climbing" runs in a rather flexible way. We too can try to adapt them to various playing situations. Here is a simple application to a ii7 / V7 / I / IV progression in G Major, using all the G Major scale tones. Notice the resolution by means of a descending pentatonic:

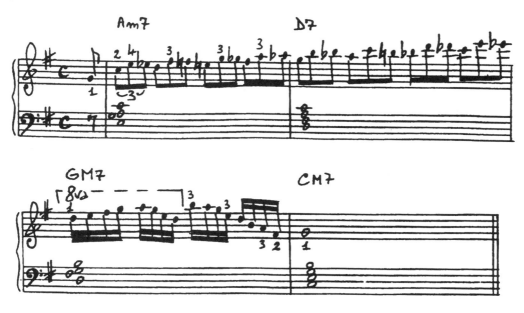

In bar 11 of "Tea for Two," Tatum played the following phrase over an Ab6 chord:

Transposed to C Major, it looks like this:

By elongating this phrase, we get a "climbing" run that can be used on Major (or relative minor) chords, as well as on ii7 / V7 / I cadences, like the one shown below:

Practice transposing the above run in all keys and in various musical situations.

The Right Hand According To Tatum

Breaks

Tatum had a special bent for playing highly imaginative breaks which often displaced the beat and/or went temporarily "outside" key. In this section, we will try to illustrate some of them.

Let's consider, first, the second break he played in his 1944 trio recording of "After You've Gone" (see the complete transcription in this book). This break falls within a V / I cadence, first "sliding" a half-tone above (i.e. Bb6 / B / Bb7 / Eb). Notice how effectively this break falls across the bars, giving rise to a wholly unexpected displacement of the beat:

A similar break (played by the right hand only) is found in bars 29-32 of this same transcription.

Another example of the many "outside" breaks Tatum used comes from the last chorus of his 1944 trio recording of "Moonglow" (also fully transcribed in this book). Notice how this break combines a "climbing" run made of four-note groups, a chromatically descending passage, then, finally, a descending arpeggio:

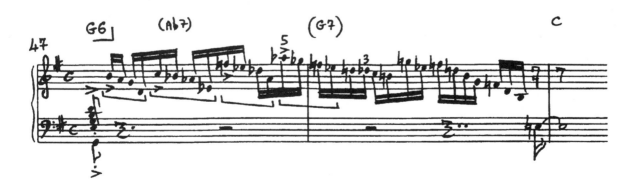

A more articulated variant of the kind of break just mentioned is found in Tatum's many memorable interpretations of "Begin the Beguine." The following example comes from bars 21-24 of the May 7, 1941 recording issued on Onyx 205. Here Tatum "slides" a half-tone below the D chord, using a "climbing" run made of groups of six notes taken from the Db Major scale. The resolution is mostly based on descending chromatic passages:

Another dissonant, "off-key" kind of break makes use of arpeggiated diminished seventh chords. See for instance the following "Ab" four-bar break from bars 13-16 of the fifth chorus of the 1945 trio recording of "Sweet Georgia Brown" (on Joker SM 3117):

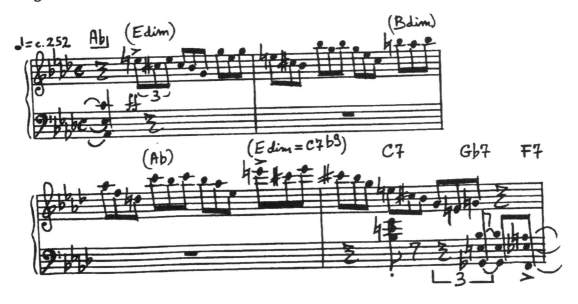

The Right Hand According To Tatum

The same idea—treated in a more adventurous rhythmic form—is found in the following break Tatum played ending the bridge of the last chorus of his 1944 solo recording of "Ain't Misbehavin'" (on the Black Lion label). See how this break uses the arpeggiated Bbdim7 and Bdim7 chords, imposed over a Bb7 chord in a V7 / I cadence:

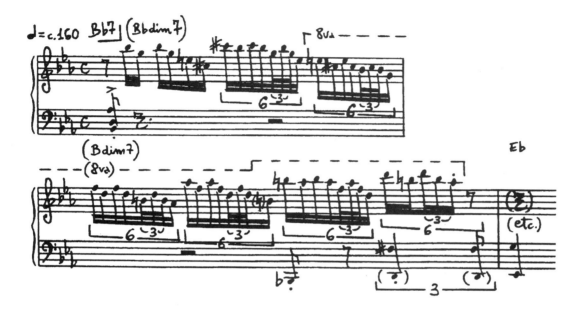

Breaks can also be played as "broken" arpeggios. See, for instance, the following example from bars 15-16 of the first chorus of "Indiana" as recorded by the Art Tatum Trio on December 20, 1952 (Capitol CDP 7 92867 2, Vols. 1 & 2):

Tatum sometimes used a very dissonant two-handed break utilizing repeated notes in triplets. The following example comes from bars 9-16 of the last chorus of the 1945 trio recording of "Sweet Georgia Brown" (on Joker SM 3117). The first four bars are a "stop time" section played by the ensemble:

In the example above, notice that starting from the third beat of bar 13 the pattern for this break alternates ascending minor 3rd skips and descending half-step movements, outlining, in effect, the two whole–tone scales:

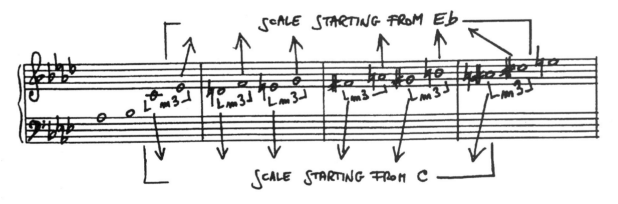

Not all of the breaks built on repeated notes in triplets adhere to the pattern we have just illustrated above. See, for instance, the following break from bars 13-16 of the third chorus of the V-Disc solo recording of "Lover" (reissued on Black Lion BLCD760114). Notice the last two bars, here outlining a C diminished chord. Also notice the alternating of single notes and octaves:

The Right Hand According To Tatum

Another kind of break favored by Tatum involved playing both hands in unison (the right hand in octaves, the left hand in single notes) in the high range of the keyboard. Good examples of this are found in the two breaks he played in the last chorus of his October 26, 1945 trio recording of "Liza" (Black Lion BLCD760114). The second break—actually a variation of the first one—features a very effective displacement of the beat in the second and third measures, with a delightful slide off the home key as the fourth measure ends:

Other remarkable break-like phrases are found in the transcription of "Indiana" in this book (see also the introductory notes to that piece).
Finally, remember that in his breaks Tatum also used his whole bag of ascending and/or descending tricks.

Classical Devices

Some of Tatum's right hand devices come from the classical piano repertoire, which he—like many other jazz pianists—studied and knew well. This chapter deals with some of the most recurrent of these devices (notice that some of these figures are actually "climbing" runs).

The next pattern is easy to understand. It is made of the G, B, and D "pivot" notes—i.e. the tones of the G Major chord, shown in circlets—embellished with their neighboring tones (the upper neighboring tones are diatonics, the lower neighboring tones are a half-tone below each "pivot"). Tatum was very fond of this device and used it very often:

Keeping the same 4-3-2-1 fingering, this figure can be easily transposed and played on the C Major and the F Major chords. With some fingering adjustments, we can also use this figure for D Major and A Major:

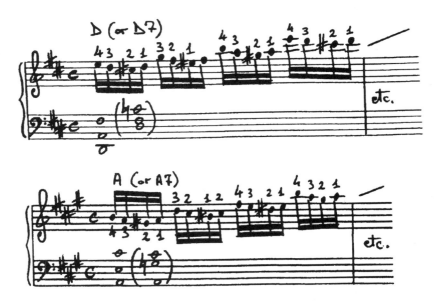

A widely used variant of this figure is shown next; it is played in triplets, omitting the first "pivot" note of each group:

A well-known classical device used by Tatum was to preface each tone of a chord with the note a half-step below it:

Another example of this comes from Tatum's 1955 private recording of "Sweet Lorraine":

This time it is played in an ascending run—taken from Tatum's recording of "St. Louis Blues":

Notice that this pattern can be easily transposed and played on most major and minor chords. Here are two examples:

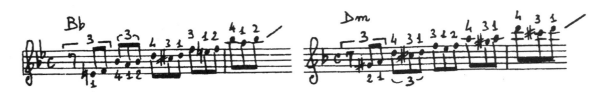

This variation comes from Tatum's famous 1933 recording of "Tiger Rag." It can be played on major and minor chords (see for instance the two examples following this figure):

Here is a possible application to a ii7 / V7 / I progression in C Major:

The Right Hand According To Tatum

"Broken" Arpeggios

One of the right hand figures Tatum was especially fond of is a particular ascending "broken" arpeggio on three-note or four-note chords:

Here is one from Tatum's recording of "Fine And Dandy."

The rule behind both patterns is to arpeggiate all the inversions of the given chord, moving upward, and omitting every third note of each inversion. Here, all the omitted tones are shown in half notes:

Tatum was very imaginative in articulating these "broken" arpeggios in different ways, using alternative rhythmic articulations as well as starting points. Following are some examples, taken from transcriptions of Tatum's playing:

("After You've Gone," bars 79-80)

("Rock Me Mama," bars 5-6):

("Ain't Misbehavin'," bar 41):

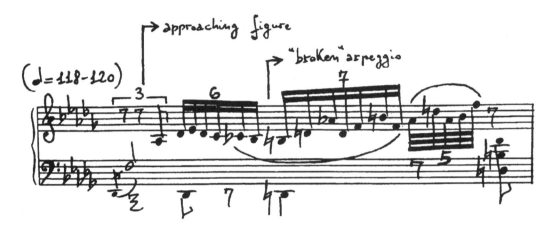

("Sweet Lorraine" bars 43-44):

("Wrap Your Troubles In Dreams," bar 30, bar 33, and bar 34):

The Right Hand According To Tatum

Concerning other possible applications of these "broken" arpeggios, it should be remembered that Tatum often built them on the upper structures of different chords, thus giving rise to more complex harmonies. The two most recurrent examples of that are the following:

(A three-note arpeggio of a chord whose root is a whole tone above the dominant seventh chord played by the left hand):

(A four-note arpeggio of a diminished seventh chord, played over a dominant seventh chord whose root is a half step below):

Other applications are possible too. Here are some, still using the ascending "broken" arpeggios of the three-note Bb Major chord and the four-note C# diminished seventh chord. Practice transposing these broken arpeggios and try to find your own applications.

"Thirds-And-Thumb"

The next figure is a basic example of one of Tatum's most dazzling right hand licks. To better understand this run, notice that the thumbs play all the notes of the C Major scale (i.e. all the white keys), while the consecutive descending thirds are built on the Db Major scale. Also, each of the "thumb" notes is a half-step below the lowest note of the next third. Notice the fingering too:

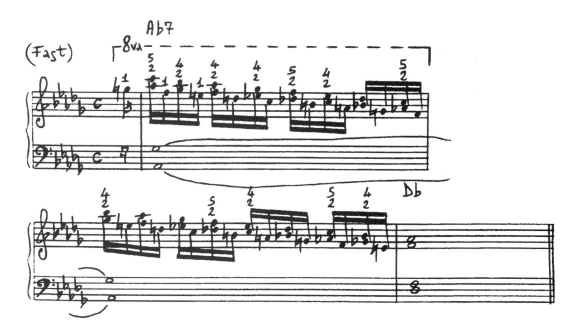

It is easy to see that this run is particularly suited to the Db Major key, hence to chords such as Db, Ab7, and Ebm7. Here is a possible application:

Very probably due to its particular configuration on the keyboard (which allows for considerable speed), Tatum did not exactly transpose this run into other keys. Rather, he seemed to use an all-purpose adjustment of this run, i.e. turning all its major thirds (or almost all of them) to minor thirds when necessary. Here is an example taken from the last chorus of the July 26, 1940 solo recording of "St. Louis Blues." Notice that the run is here played in the key of D minor:

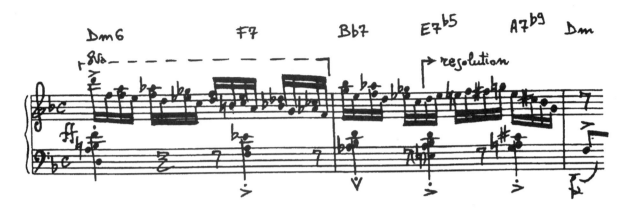

Another example comes from "Moonglow." Here the run is played on a G7 chord and all of its thirds are minor thirds:

The third example comes from bar 21 of "Esquire Bounce." The run is here played in a shortened form on an F7 chord:

Judging from the examples above, we may presume that Tatum intended this kind of run almost as a brush-stroke of sound, often without a specific relation to the underlying chords. This run was extensively used by the late, great Dick Wellstood, and was also a trademark (though in a simplified and slightly different form) of the old stride pianist Cliff Jackson.[1]

Other jazz pianists have played a simplified adaptation—in single notes—of this Tatum run, by eliminating all the upper notes of the consecutive thirds. The following example is an excerpt from "Rosetta," as recorded by Teddy Wilson in April 1941. Here again see that all the "thumb" notes outline the C Major scale, while all the other notes come from the Db Major scale:

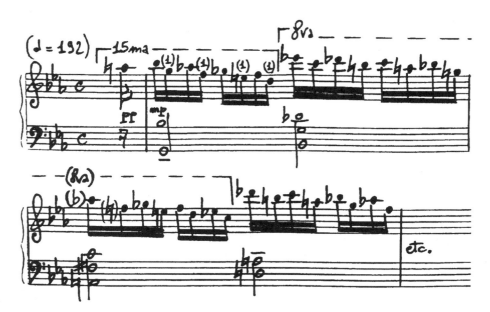

[1]See, for instance, the transcriptions of "Royal Garden Blues," "Crazy Rhythm," and "Happy Birthday To Pat" in Harlem Stride Piano Solos published by Ekay Music and the transcription of "If Dreams Come True" in Dick Wellstood Jazz Piano Solos (San Diego, California, Neil A. Kjos Music Company, 1994), both collections transcribed and annotated by Riccardo Scivales.

Finally, here is yet another variant, found in bars 64-66 of Tatum's own composition "Turquoise." Notice that in this run all the "thumb" notes still come from the C Major scale, while all the other notes outline the Eb Major—or Bb7 Mixolydian—scale (the only exception to this is the first G, which is flat). Also notice that many of the triplets are actually played in single notes. The fingering here is our suggestion:

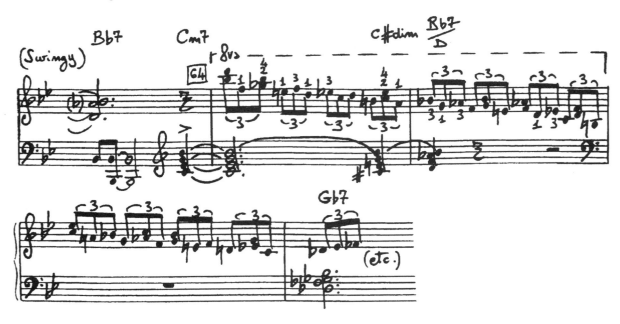

Here is a possible application to a ii7 / V7 / I progression in Eb (remember that you can substitute any of the thirds with a single note—i.e., the lowest note of that third—played with your third finger):

Runs Beginning With Repeated Six-Note Figures

When playing very fast tempos, one of the most spectacular of Tatum's devices was to close his solos with a long, breathtaking run in triplets, beginning with a six-note repeated figure and continuing with descending chromatic movement—interrupted by a few ascending skips—before resolving into fragments of the descending pentatonic major scale. Tatum loved this device and used it often. A beautiful example is found in bars 5-8 of the third chorus of the 1945 group recording of "I Got Rhythm" (transcribed in this book):

A similar run—initiated by a slightly different six-note repeated figure—is found in bars 61-64 of "Mop Mop." The resolution is different too, but the basic concept is the same. Notice that in "I Got Rhythm" this run was played on a C7 / F7 / Bb cadence, whereas in "Mop Mop" the run was played on the Bb7 / Eb / E dim / Bb / F7 / Bb changes:

Another example comes from the bridge of the last chorus of Tatum's trio recording of "Liza" (October 26, 1945):

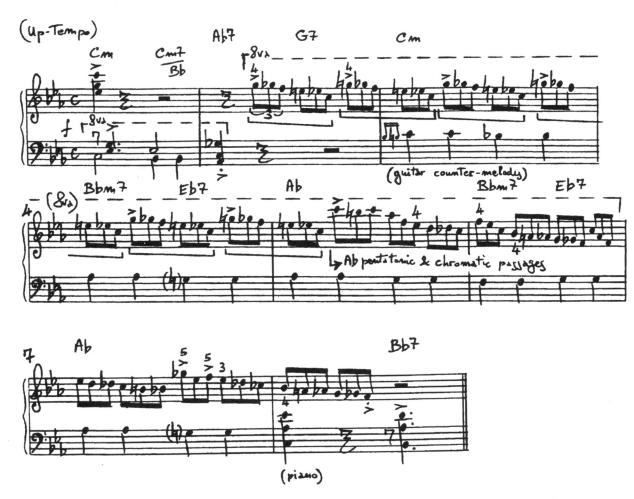

(Note: In bars 3-7 of the above example Tatum does not play anything with his left hand, so we have included the guitar counter-melody played by Tiny Grimes.)

Repeated "Jam-Like" Figures

During his solos, Tatum often used a variety of repeated six-note figures which fell across the bar lines and almost seemed to "jam." These figures are very effective when played—as Tatum did them—at fast tempos. See, for instance, the following example, taken from Tatum's 1945 recording of "Runnin' Wild," issued on Black Lion BLP 30124. These four bars are a break, with the jam-like figure resolved by a five-note run on the C7 chord:

Another example comes from Tatum's 1944 recording of his own composition, "Gang O'Notes" (on Black Lion BLP 30124). Notice that the repeated jam-like figure is here played on a minor chord, with a descending chromatic resolution:

Tatum used many different varieties of these figures. The next example is found in a Tatum recording of "I Know That You Know," transcribed by Jed Distler in the magazine *Keyboard Classics*, March/April 1990:

The six-note jamming figure can also begin on the 5th of a dominant seventh chord, as found in the 1955 solo recording of "Moonglow":

Playing repeated groupings of six notes—which create a polyrhythm within binary time signatures—is a well-known stride, blues, and jazz cliché. One of the earliest and best piano examples is found in the second chorus of "Numb Fumblin'," composed and recorded in 1929 by Thomas "Fats" Waller, one of the foremost sources of inspiration for Tatum. Here is an excerpt from my book, *Harlem Stride Piano Solos*, published by Ekay Music:

By inserting a triplet in the repeated six-note figure, we have a seven-note jam-like figure, as in the following excerpt from Tatum's composition, "Amethyst":

You can apply these figures in many ways. Here is an example using the last four bars of a blues chorus in C, where a figure from "Gang O'Notes" has been adapted to the G7 and F7 chords—and then resolved with a descending five-note run on the C7 chord:

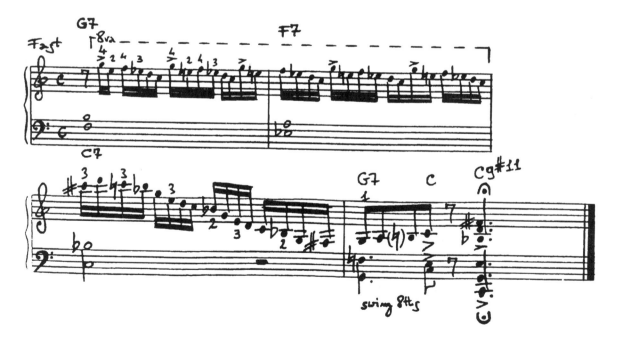

Reshaping And Adapting A Basic Idea

Tatum had an outstanding skill in tirelessly reshaping a basic idea, adapting it to various musical situations. This was one of the most distinctive and significant aspects of his improvisational language. In this chapter we will discuss some of his creative reworkings of one of his most recurrent right hand figures on the V7 / I (or ii7 / V7 / I) cadence in G. The basic idea we are taking into consideration is the figure Tatum played in bar 17 of his piano solo on "Mop Mop":

By comparing this figure with bars 21-22 and 13-14 of "Moonglow," we can see Tatum's mastery in continuously reshaping one idea—by giving it different starting points, rhythmic articulations, and resolutions, as well as by omitting and/or changing a few notes:

"Moonglow," bars 21-22

"Moonglow," bars 13-14

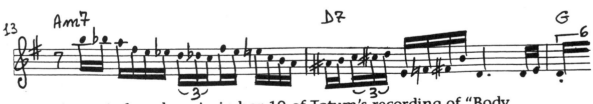

The same figure is found again in bar 10 of Tatum's recording of "Body And Soul":

Let's concentrate on this last figure. First, it can be easily transposed and played on other chords:

We can vary its applications, too. For instance, play this figure on ii7 / V7 changes in place of just the V7 chord. See the following example, where it has been inserted in a whole turnaround in F Major:

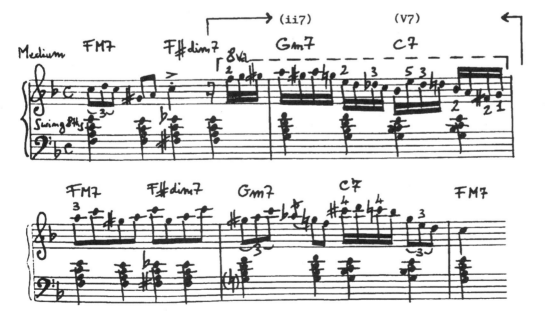

As usual, we can mix this figure with other Tatum runs, to get a longer line:

Or we might choose to play repeated sequences of this figure on a circle of
fifths progression:

Listen to how Tatum unceasingly reshaped and adapted the same basic figures throughout his recordings, and find your own adaptations too. Here are two further examples of Tatum's skill in reshaping the runs above. Here it is on an A7 chord in bars 13-14 of his December 20, 1952 trio recording of "Indiana" (on Capitol CDP 7 92867 2, Vols. 1 & 2):

And here is how he played it in bars 17-20 of the January 5, 1944 trio recording of "I Got Rhythm":

Tatum's Improvisatory Approach

Art Tatum was perhaps one of the most enigmatic and elusive of jazz improvisers, because his improvisations were generally devoid of a conventional (i.e. "singable") melodic quality, and were filled with chromatic and/or "outside" passages which puzzle the average listener. In addition, he used to elaborate his most recognizable runs, licks, and phrases in an always changing and most astonishing way. Like a master juggler, in the space of a few bars he was able to hurl several musical ideas one behind the other, often bewildering the listener with complex and wholly unexpected solutions played at a fantastic speed.

Certain recurrent features of his improvisatory approach come quite clearly out of his recorded legacy (on this matter, also see the introductory notes to the solos in this book):

• even in the statements of song themes, he usually gave the listener just a few basic hints of the original melodies. Brief melodic statements or tortuous chromatic paraphrases of the original themes, in fact, were alternated with distinctive runs or with enterprising passages in triplets or double-time phrasing (often using dissonant, altered, and jangling skips);

• runs, licks, and other figures are often connected to form longer and more complex lines;

• rests are rarely used;

• especially at fast tempos, Tatum played long, uninterrupted lines without any reference to the original melody;

• frequent quotations from the classical, popular, and jazz repertory are interpolated within the improvisations;

• the harmonic foundation is very sophisticated and highly chromatic, with an extensive use of substitute and altered chords, passing harmonies, and complete reharmonizations. On this matter, Dick Hyman has written that in his opinion "the advances in harmony of the boppers were simplistic compared to Tatum's usage."[1] Indeed, by the late thirties Tatum had developed an exceptionally modern harmonic language, using practically the entire tonal palette (and later using impressionistic devices as well).

[1]Dick Hyman. *Piano Pro*. Ekay Music, 1992, p. 26.

Some of the above-mentioned features of Tatum's improvisational language are summarized in the following eight bars from the first chorus of his 1945 solo recording of "Memories of You" (on Black Lion BLP 30124)—which also is a good example of his approach to ballads. See the paraphrase of the original theme in triplets (bars 1-2), the short and syncopated melodic statement beginning bar 5, the double-time phrases played in bars 3 and 7, and the connecting runs (fourth beat of bar 5-bar 6, and bar 8). Also notice that the run played in bar 8 is actually made of two distinctive runs (i.e. the "climbing" run—first two beats—and the descending "four-note" run on the G7b9 chord), connected to each other by the chromatic passage on the third beat:

Another representative example of Tatum's approach—this time at medium tempo—is found in bars 9-16 of the second chorus of his 1944 great solo recording of "Ain't Misbehavin'" (on Black Lion BLP 30203). Here, too, he gives the listener just a hint of "conventional" melody (see the paraphrase of the theme in bars 9-11). Then he plays an outstanding five-bar long complex phrase in double-time. Let's see how this phrase is built. It starts with an Eb descending pentatonic (bar 12), developed with descending chromatic passages and some skips (bar 13), a brief "outside" arpeggio on the B7 chord, more descending chromatics, and an arpeggio on the Bb7 chord (bar 14). At this point (opening of bar 15), the phrase seems concluded, but Tatum throws it again with the ascending scale played by the left hand, resolved by the right hand with a chromatic fragment leading to the descending four-note run on the G7b9 chord (bar 16). A few chromatic adjustments finally land him on the essential tones of the next chord (i.e. Cm, beginning of the bridge). The chord symbols here report the chord changes actually played by Tatum's left hand:

As a whole, the five-bar long phrase we have just discussed above is an eloquent example of how Tatum's improvisatory language was largely based on his skill in developing his distinctive runs and connecting them together in various ways. As proof of this, we can compare bars 13-16 of the example above with the symmetrical episode found in the third chorus of the same recording. Here Tatum starts playing the Eb descending penta-tonic scale. Then, in bar 14 a few descending chromatics and a figure on the Bb7 chord lead to the left hand ascending scale, this time resolved by the ascending "broken" arpeggio (right hand) on the G7b9 chord (also notice that the measure in 7/8 time is clearly played that way):

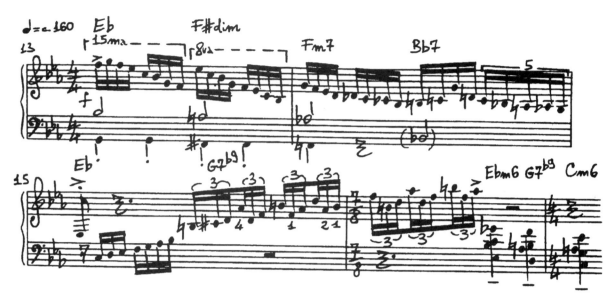

Especially when improvising at fast tempos with his trio or other groups, Tatum often reduced his left hand role to a sparse bop-like one, his right hand playing long, uninterrupted descending lines without any reference to the original song themes. Many of the most impressive among these long lines were actually based on his descending pentatonic scales and five-note or four-note runs on dominant seventh chords, wildly transfigured by the insertion of descending chromatic passing tones as well as by some ascending skips (whose function was to "gain" keys in order to further elongate these phrases). Some good examples of this improvisatory approach are found in the 1945 trio recording of "Sweet Georgia Brown" reissued on Joker SM 3117. In the three examples below, we have transcribed some of these long phrases, giving the chord symbols for the basic changes played by the trio. The arrows indicate the starting points of the runs used as the basis of these long lines (you will easily recognize the ascending skips and the descending chromatic passing tones interspersed throughout):

("Sweet Georgia Brown," 1st chorus, bars 21-24):

("Sweet Georgia Brown," 5th chorus, bars 17-20):

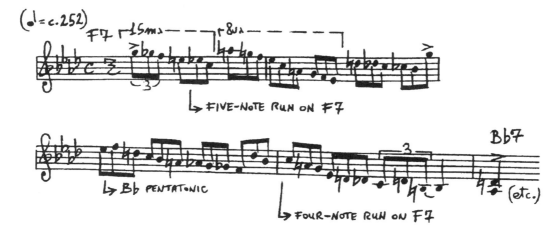

("Sweet Georgia Brown," 2nd chorus, bars 13-17):

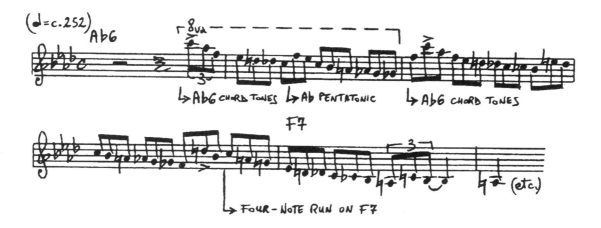

Over the years, a notorious dispute has arisen about the skills of Art Tatum as a jazz improviser. On the pretext that he sometimes recorded similar versions of his "set" arrangements of certain songs[2] (using many of his distinctive runs), some critics and jazz historians claim that he could not be considered a real and spontaneous jazz improviser. This seems to be a very hasty and inattentive conclusion indeed. It is undeniable that Tatum sometimes recorded similar or almost identical versions of pieces, including "Tea for Two," "Begin the Beguine," and the trio arrangement of "Liza." On the other hand, he also left us plenty of very different versions of the same pieces. We might consider the alternate takes of "After You've Gone" or "Liza" reissued on MCA GRP 16072, or the two versions of "Sweet Lorraine" which have been brilliantly transcribed and annotated by Jed Distler in his Art Tatum book (published by Music Sales Corp.). These and countless other examples witness the greatness of Tatum as a master of jazz improvisation.

As far as his recurrent use of particular and preconceived figures and runs, they simply were an integral and functional part of his improvisational language. As we have seen throughout this book, he tirelessly reshaped and elaborated these runs. Every jazz improviser has his own repertory of distinctive licks and phrases. Perhaps the problem with Tatum's runs is that they are so showy and "melodic"—i.e. easier to be noticed and retained by the average listener and critic. In this perspective, Tatum's detractors should pay more attention to the phrases he played between his runs. On this matter, Dick Hyman has most aptly observed that Tatum "combined the basic vocabulary of his runs and scales so that they were never textbook exercises. His linear improvisation developed from this constant reconstituting of his material."[3]

We think this Dick Hyman observation is fundamental to the way you can use the repertory of runs and phrases illustrated in this book. Learn them in all the applicable keys, with variants. Then, find your own solutions for how to develop and elaborate (or even transform) them. Finally, practice connecting them in as many ways as possible, to create longer lines within the harmonic framework commonly found in jazz music. Further inspiration, of course, will come from the transcribed solos included in the next pages of this book.

[2]On this matter, it is worth noting that these recorded "set" arrangements sound similar in texture and development, but they actually feature many different (and extemporaneous) passages, choices of notes, left hand work, etc. (as if Tatum were improvising within the overall structures of his "set" arrangements). It is likely that he intended these arrangements as "ideal," perfect versions of certain songs, resulting from his constant performance of them over the years.

[3]Dick Hyman. Piano Pro. Ekay Music, 1992

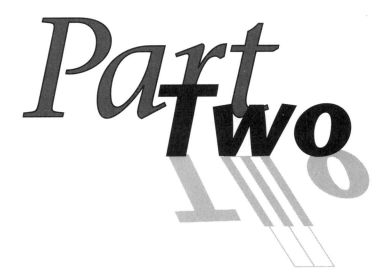

Part Two

Transcribed Solos

(with introductory notes)

"After You've Gone"

This beautiful interpretation with plenty of swing was recorded on January 5, 1944 by the Art Tatum trio with Tiny Grimes (guitar) and slam Stewart (double bass and vocal effects). (This was Tatum's first trio, formed in 1943 and active during the Forties. In the early Fifties Tatum had another trio, with Everett Barksdale on guitar and still Slam Stewart (or Bill Pemberton) on string bass. This trio has left us some quite rare and truly outstanding recordings now reissued on the indispensable Capitol CDP 7 (92867 2, Vol. 1 & 2).

Tatum plays in a linear way, limiting his left hand role to the statement of the original chord changes, mostly following this simple and bebop-like rhythmic pattern:

Also notice that many of the left hand chords he played in this piece are modern "rootless" chords (see for instance bars 23-27 and 50-51).

Transcribed here are the Intro and Tatum's two solo choruses, i.e., the first and the fourth one of this recording (the other two solo choruses, as usual, were taken by Grimes and by Stewart). Many interesting Tatum devices are found throughout this interpretation of "After You've Gone":

• the beautiful phrase played in bars 23-24 on a G7 chord leading to a C Major chord (a V7 / I cadence). The pattern of this phrase can be transposed and used in ii7 / V7 / I cadences. Here is an example in D Major (practice transposing in other keys as well):

In his January 5, 1944 trio recording of "I Got Rhythm," Tatum played this very same figure, changing just the first note and the resolution:

• the very effective "outside" (i.e. shifting a half-tone above) breaks played in bars 29-32 and 53-56.

• the four-bar long phrase found in bars 35-38. We can see it as follows: 1) Ebm6 chord tones, connected by chromatic notes; 2) Bb pentatonic run; 3) chromatic resolution:

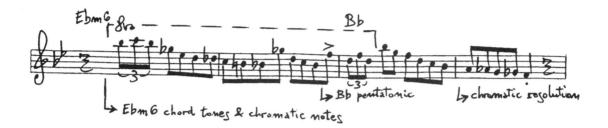

• even longer (and much more adventurous) is the astounding phrase played in bars 45-52. Notice that it starts with the "climbing" run previously discussed.

At the end of the string bass/vocal effects solo chorus by Slam Stewart, Tatum plays one of his distinctive descending four-note runs on a dominant seventh chord, thus flowing into the fourth and last chorus (bar 57 onwards). The main feature of the first half of this chorus is the long series of tenths in the bass (another of his favorite devices). Also notice that in bars 70-75 these tenths are split between the two hands. This episode was probably conceived in order to create contrast with the final part of this chorus (bar 76 onwards), which is again based on a "linear" right hand phrasing and a "horizontal" conception. In bars 80-81 we find the distinctive "broken" arpeggio figure. The overwhelming finale is taken in the spirited "shout" vein which was peculiar to stride pianists like James P. Johnson and Thomas "Fats" Waller (both of whom, we know, were crucial in the development of Tatum's style). Last but not least, notice that the concluding phrase played in bars 98-99 has become a cliché used by many other jazzmen after Tatum. It is based on the descending pentatonic major scale, and its pattern is easy to see. You can transpose it in various other keys. Here is an example in Eb:

After You've Gone

as recorded by Art Tatum on January 5, 1944

Henry Creamer and Turner Layton
Transcribed by Riccardo Scivales

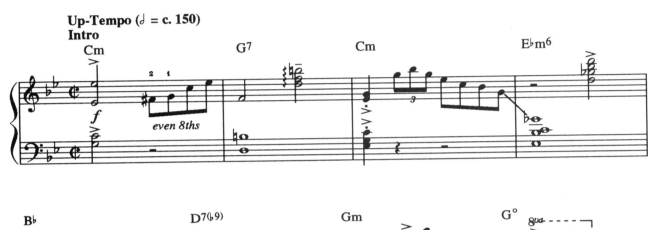

The Right Hand According To Tatum

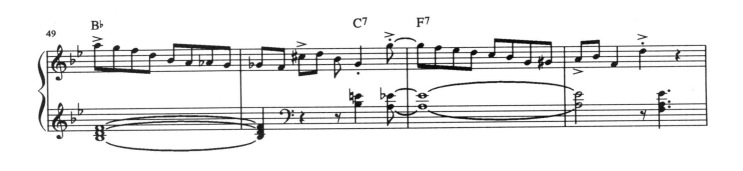

(2nd Chorus)

The Right Hand According To Tatum

(R.H. run introducing the 4th chorus)

4th Chorus

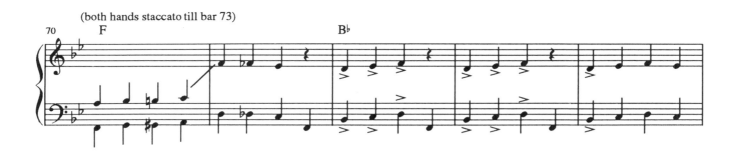

(both hands staccato till bar 73)

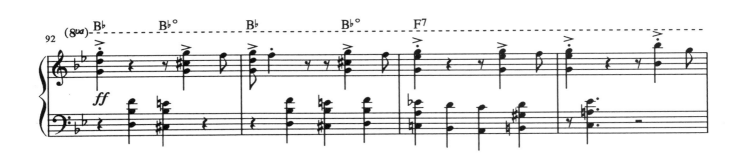

The Right Hand According To Tatum

"Esquire Bounce"

Like "Mop Mop" (also transcribed in this book), "Esquire Bounce" was recorded at The Metropolitan Opera House on January 18, 1944 and is one of Tatum's most famous group recordings. In this book's perspective, "Esquire Bounce" is also important because during his piano solo chorus, Tatum made extensive use of his distinctive right hand devices, such as:

• the descending pentatonic runs of bars 2 and 19-20;

• in bars 7-8, a variant of the descending pentatonic run, enriched by means of chromatic passing tones (notice that this run is played on a I / VI7 / II7 / V7 / I turnaround in Eb Major):

• the "climbing" run of bars 5-6;

• the dissonant, slash-like lick previously discussed (bars 11-12):

• the "climbing" run in four-note groups found in bars 17-18;

• a hint of the "Thirds-And-Thumb" run (bar 21);

• the sparkling lick of bars 26-27;

• the conclusive long phrase in triplets starting in bar 29.

Due to the accompaniment of guitar and string-bass, as well as to the low sound quality of this recording, in some passages Tatum's left hand work is barely audible. For this reason, in bars 1-4 and 9-14 of our transcription the left hand part is an adaptation of what is actually played by Tatum.

Esquire Bounce

as recorded by Art Tatum on January 18, 1944

Leonard Feather

Transcribed by Riccardo Scivales

The Right Hand According To Tatum

"I Got Rhythm" And The Modern "Horn-Like" Melodic Approach

This version of "I Got Rhythm" was recorded in 1945 by Tatum with a group including Roy Eldridge and Charlie Shavers (trumpets), Vic Dickenson and Benny Morton (trombones), Ben Webster (tenor sax), Edmund Hall (clarinet), Slam Stewart (string bass), and Sidney Catlett (drums).

Transcribed here is the Tatum piano solo (i.e. the second chorus of this recording). Since he makes extremely sparse use of the left hand, we have transcribed his right hand improvisation only. The chord symbols are provided just as a basic reference of the many harmonic variants of this song. Both "Mop Mop" (also transcribed in this book) and "I Got Rhythm" are based on practically the same chord changes, so it is interesting to compare Tatum's solos on these two pieces.

Some of Tatum's improvisational devices in this solo on "I Got Rhythm" are as follows:

• in bars 2-3, 13-14, and 29-30 (as well as in bars 2 and 45 of "Mop Mop"), see the recurrent figure built on Bb Major chord tones, shown below in circlets (also remember that this figure is easily transposable in C, Db, Eb, F, G, Ab, and B Major):

Notice how Tatum gives different resolutions to the figure mentioned above, playing it on different chords and starting from different points. Here are some examples from the above mentioned bars of "I Got Rhythm" and "Mop Mop":

(Further examples of Tatum's adaptations of this basic figure are found in the January 5, 1944 Tatum trio recording of "I Got Rhythm":

• in bars 5-6, we can see that the lick in triplets is an adaptation of the early figure we studied at the beginning of this book. The pattern can be transposed to C, Db, D, Eb, F, G, Ab, and A. Here is an example in C:

• in bars 9-10, Tatum plays his distinctive "climbing" run already shown. Notice the resolution, based on descending chromatic notes (bar 11) and the Bb pentatonic run (bar 12).

In the bridge of this chorus, Slam Stewart plays a string bass solo (here the piano comps). Tatum resumes his solo in bar 25. Notice the "outside" passage played in bars 28-29.

In this recording of "I Got Rhythm," Tatum took another solo in the bridge of the third chorus (also included in our transcription). The last four bars of this bridge feature one of Tatum's most impressive and recurrent devices: a six-note repeated figure resolved with descending chromatic passages, ascending skips, and the descending pentatonic run corresponding to the tonic key (here, Bb). Tatum loved to conclude his solos with this whirling device (see for instance the last four bars of our transcription of "Mop Mop"), which you can try on your own in different situations and keys. A very interesting aspect of this run is that it is applied in different harmonic situations, i.e. C7 / F7 in "I Got Rhythm" and Bb7 / Eb / Edim / Bb / F7 / Bb in "Mop Mop." It is apparent that Tatum here thinks in purely "horizontal" melodic terms related to the tonic key, as if he were disregarding the chord changes (i.e., in his improvisation he seems to focus on the tonic key scale—or the pentatonic scale corresponding to it—rather than on the chord tones of each isolated chord). This melodic approach (associated with the horn phrasing of modern jazz at fast tempos) seems not to have been used by any pianist prior to Tatum, and it is another remarkably innovative aspect of his art.

I Got Rhythm

as recorded by Art Tatum, 1945

Music and Lyrics by George Gershwin and Ira Gershwin
Transcribed by Riccardo Scivales

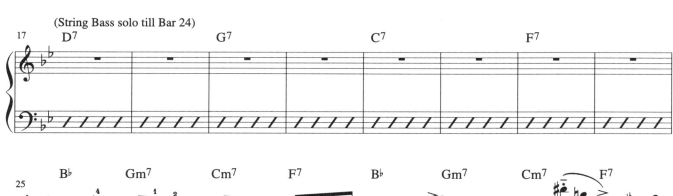

(String Bass solo till Bar 24)

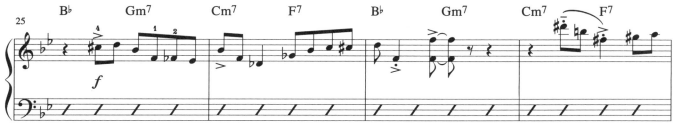

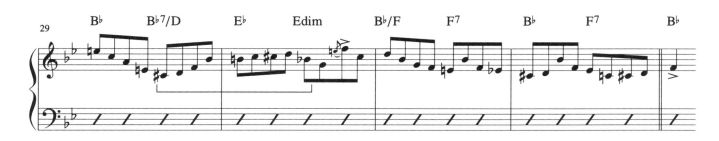

Bridge of 3rd Chorus:

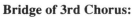

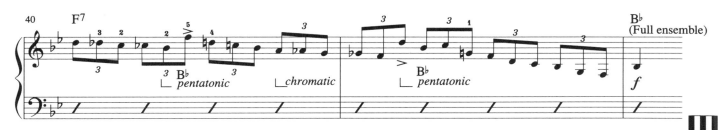

"Indiana"

The great Art Tatum was famous for his amazing technical command. His unique, legendary skill in playing is reflected in performances of the most lightning-fast tempos (♩ = 320 and even greater speeds were easy for him). Yet many of his masterwork recordings were taken at a more relaxed pace, which allows us to have a closer look at his style.

An example is his piano solo interpretation of "Indiana," recorded on July 26, 1940, and played in a very relaxed mood at medium tempo. This piano solo consists of an eight-bar intro and two choruses. We have transcribed the first chorus.

Dressed up with a lush reharmonization, including plenty of altered, passing and substitute chords, the first chorus of Tatum's "Indiana" is a beautiful paraphrase of the original theme. Luckily, it also features quite a number of Tatum's characteristic devices and right-hand runs. What follows is a catalog of some of them:

In bar 4, Tatum plays one of his descending four-note runs, built on the tones of an A9 chord (the tonic is played in the bass only). This is one of the most recurrent Tatum devices. A similar run is used to close the phrase in bar 8 (also, notice how Tatum resolves both these runs to reach the third of the next chord).

In Bars 5-6 feature an enterprisingly "modern" yet melodically delicious paraphrase in triplets, based on some passing chords from D7 to G. This articulated kind of phrasing, with unusual skips and displaced accents, is also a typical Tatum device.

In bar 7, Tatum plays a very fast "climbing" run built around the tones of a G Major chord. Often used by him, this is a well-known device from the classical piano literature, which Tatum studied and knew well. (Also, notice that bars 7-8 as a whole can be considered a "break" phrase to fill the "rest" space of the original melody.)

In bars 15-16, we find another "climbing" figure made of four-note groups taken from the Db Major scale and played upon a D9 chord. So, this phrase goes temporarily "outside"—i.e. a half-step lower—the harmony, finally reaching the G Major tonic chord by means of plenty of chromaticism:

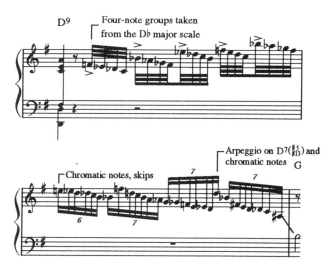

Bars 19-23 feature an adventurous double-time phrase played in "Swing 16ths," with an interesting use of altered and chromatic tones:

Note the fourth beat of bar 23-bar 24: a lightning-like and "climbing" broken arpeggio made of the tones of a diminished seventh chord. Tatum was very fond of this device, often found in the classical literature, too.

In bar 25 Tatum plays one of his distinctive pentatonic runs using the pentatonic major scale of G. Notice the "approaching" chromatic tones—most of the Tatum pentatonic runs are approached in a similar way, and they are often resolved with some chromatic notes leading to the next chord or phrase. By means of alternating skips, chromatic passages, and descending runs, Tatum was able to create very agile and interesting phrases. Bar 8 is a brief yet clear example of that (a more extended application of this concept eventually led to the innovative long phrases often found in Tatum's later recordings).

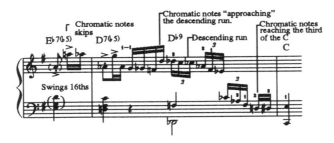

Beyond their self-evident technical mastery, the astounding thing about the Tatum runs illustrated above is that they are played with a very precise rhythmic subdivision—they are not mere ornamentation, but the substance of part of his musical language—which also holds the key to how to start practicing them. One important aspect of the accompaniment: in bars 1 and 12 we find the so-called "clipped-bass note" technique; that is, left-hand tenths whose lower notes are played like grace notes.

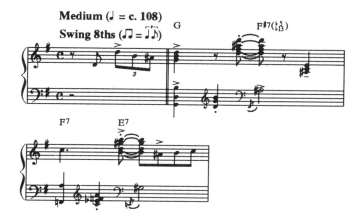

In the second chorus of "Indiana"—not transcribed here—Tatum plays two adventurous break-like phrases. The first one, found in bars 39-40, is based on a I/IV situation with many passing chords:

The second break-like phrase comes from bars 47-48, in a V7 / bII7 / I cadence starting on a whole-tone scale:

Despite the deep admiration of most musicians, Tatum's achievements and influence on the evolution of jazz were overlooked by some critics and historians, who disliked his virtuosity and accused him of lacking real inventiveness. Judging by this 1940 recording of "Indiana," it is indeed evident that at that time, Tatum was already in complete command of a remarkably advanced musical language, rich in innovative devices commonly associated with later jazz styles.

Indiana

as recorded by Art Tatum on July 26, 1940

Ballard MacDonard and James F. Hanley
Transcribed by Riccardo Scivales

"Knockin' Myself Out"

Among other things, Tatum was famous for his legendary "after-hours" sessions, in which it is said he played in a most spontaneous, informal, and experimental way (also singing in some pieces, such as "Toledo Blues"). With portable equipment in 1941, Jerry Newman recorded some of these sessions at the Gee-Haw Stables, Reuben's and Clark Monroe's Uptown House Harlem clubs. Among these recordings is "Knockin' Myself Out," a blues piece Tatum played with bassist/singer Chocolate Williams on July 26, 1941 at the Gee-Haw Stables. Besides singing on some choruses, in "Knockin' Myself Out" Tatum played the two full solo piano choruses we have transcribed here. They are the first and the eighth choruses, marked by a very relaxed and informal mood, with sparse left hand work (in bars 6-11 and 13-15, the left hand part is just our suggestion, provided for harmonic reference).

As a whole, in "Knockin' Myself Out" Tatum used both a traditional bluesy phrasing and some of his distinctive and more advanced devices. The first chorus is basically traditional, further proving that Tatum was an able and "real" blues player despite some critics' incredible assertions. In bar 2, notice the subtle and effective idea of alternating a triplet, a sextuplet, and a triplet again.

The eighth chorus is more adventurous and experimental, and it is also one of Tatum's most astonishing exploits. In bar 15, he plays the distinctive, dissonant trick we studied earlier. Bars 17-18 are a little jewel of inventiveness and enterprise. After placing a totally unexpected and effective C9b5 left hand chord, Tatum plays a lightning-like descending-ascending phrase split between the hands and resolved by one of his descending runs on an F7 chord. You are advised to listen to this recording (available on Onyx 205CD) to fully appreciate this episode in all its acrobatic beauty.

In bars 20-21 we find one of Tatum's diatonic-chromatic ascending runs, whose pattern is shown below (diatonics in whole notes, chromatics in small black notes). It is discussed in the chapter on "climbing" runs:

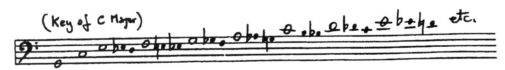

The eighth chorus ends with a blues-stride phrase in James P. Johnson's manner (bar 23), followed by one of Tatum's two-handed tricks. Again it must be noted that when accompanying the vocal choruses of "Knockin' Myself Out," he played the purest of blues piano. His accompaniments here are never intrusive, and he truly uses a wide repertoire of traditional blues piano devices. During his after-hours sessions in clubs like Clark Monroe's, it is unlikely that Tatum was not heard by younger jazzmen and future boppers, who probably had the chance to absorb the more advanced aspects of his style, such as the double-time phrasing and the harmonic innovations. On this matter, also see the introductory notes to "Sweet Georgia Brown."

Knockin' Myself Out

as recorded by Art Tatum on July 26, 1941

Lil Green

Transcribed by Riccardo Scivales

^aVery probably by mistake, bassist Chocolate Williams interprets the first eight bars as a piano Intro, thus entering at bar 9 with a walking bass line on the C6 chord.

"Moonglow": The "Linear" and "Melodious" Tatum

Recorded on January 5, 1944 with guitarist Tiny Grimes and bassist Slam Stewart, "Moonglow" is one of the most perfect, delightful, and swinging creations of Tatum's first trio. It is also one of the best examples of what we might call the "linear" and "melodious" Tatum. In this interpretation he played in a very "horizontal" and melodic way, reducing the role of his left hand to the essential (in a way that foretells bebop piano), while also staying close to the original chord changes of this song without overcomplicating them with his more customary substitutions and passing chords. Thus, "Moonglow" is an excellent chance to focus on Tatum's right hand work (this also could be the easiest-to-play solo in the book).

This recording follows the most usual four-choruses-scheme adopted by the Tatum Trio, that is: Intro, 1st chorus (piano paraphrase of the theme), 2nd chorus (guitar solo), 3rd chorus (string bass and vocal effects solo), 4th chorus (piano solo and/or paraphrase). We have transcribed the Intro and the full first and fourth choruses.

Quite a number of Tatum's distinctive right hand devices are featured in this solo. In the first chorus, see for instance:

• the descending pentatonic runs in bars 11 and 23;

• bars 13-14 and 21-22: the sparkling double-tempo phrases played on ii7 / V7 / I cadences. Both these phrases are variations of Tatum's recurrent idea;

• bars 17-20 and 33-36: the graceful paraphrase of the theme in triplets. This kind of paraphrasing—based on arpeggios on sixth and thirteenth chords—actually recalls the style of the stride pianist Willie "The Lion" Smith, one of Tatum's foremost mentors;

• bars 30-31 we find a characteristic "climbing" break-like phrase made of rhythmically displaced groups of four notes. Another kind of "climbing" break (with a descending resolution) is played in bars 15-16 (also see the chapter "Breaks" in this book);

• bar 32 features a descending arpeggio outlining a G7b5 chord—due to the well-known rule of tritone substitutions, this same figure can of course be played on a Db7b5 chord too;

• bar 37 shows an application of a run previously discussed in this book.

The Right Hand According To Tatum

As to the fourth and last chorus (bar 41 onwards in the transcription), it is similar to the first one in its overall conception and development (see for instance the descending pentatonics, the paraphrases in triplets, and the break-like phrase in bars 47-48). Among the main points of interest in this chorus are:

- the sparkling application of the very first figure we studied in bar 54;

- the very spectacular descending pentatonic run played on an E7 chord in bars 60-61, filling the entire range of the keyboard;

- the very adventurous and modern phrase played on a II7 / V7 / I cadence in C Major (bars 64-66), truly advanced for jazz in 1944:

(As a very good exercise, you could practice transposing the above phrase to other keys.)

Notice: Ending the piece (bars 77-79), Tatum plays an extended descending pentatonic run, which is not wholly audible because of the phrase played by the guitar at the same time. So we have concluded the transcription with that guitar phrase (to be played by both hands in unison).

Moonglow

as recorded by Art Tatum on January 5, 1944

Words and Music by Will Hudson, Eddie DeLange and Irving Mills
Transcribed by Riccardo Scivales

The Right Hand According To Tatum

"Mop Mop"

"Mop Mop" is one of the best and most celebrated group recordings of Tatum. It was recorded on January 18, 1944 during a famous concert held at New York's Metropolitan Opera House, gathering great jazzmen like Louis Armstrong, Roy Eldridge, Coleman Hawkins, Barney Bigard, Jack Teagarden, Al Casey, Oscar Pettiford, Sidney Catlett and others (all these musicians played together for this piece).

A typical vehicle for jam sessions, "Mop Mop" is also important because the improvisations on it are built on practically the same chord changes as "I Got Rhythm"–that is, the so-called "rhythm changes" which along with the 12-bar blues form is the most widely used in jazz.[1] During his solos on "Mop Mop," Tatum made very sparse and bebop-like use of the left hand, mostly playing just a few isolated rootless chords from time to time, thus leaving a lot of bars unaccompanied by his left hand. The accompaniment played by guitar and double bass here seems mostly improvised and not planned in advance—in various passages, it seems that the guitar and the string bass do not play the same chord together. However, as a general harmonic reference for the improvisation on "Mop Mop" we can take the chord changes reported in our transcription.[2]

Tatum's first two solo choruses[3] on "Mop Mop," transcribed here, are very interesting. In some passages he took many liberties with the chord changes, almost as if he had decided to disregard them and to impose his own phrases over them. See, for instance, bars 9-16 where he plays a very long run in triplets, almost exclusively made of arpeggios on diminished seventh chords,[4] resulting in the harmonic clashes found in bars 10-15. Consider also the astounding and rather odd idea of bars 25-30, where we find him playing one of his favorite "tricks," that is a very fast series of hammered (tremolo-like) octaves and single notes, structured on the following pattern in ascending minor 3rd skips and descending half-note skips:

The other important Tatum devices found in this transcription are:

• the beautiful long phrase in triplets in bars 17-19. As previously noted in this book, this phrase is a reshaping of a recurrent basic idea;

• the "three-over-four" phrase in bars 34-35;

• bar 39: the distinctive right hand "broken" arpeggio;

• bars 42-44: the interesting episode built on dissonant slash-like licks with a very strong displacement of the beat;

• in bars 49-55 the left hand claims a role, playing a long series of melodic tenths which were often used by Tatum on secondary dominant seventh chords;

• the delicious bluesy riff in bars 57-60;

• bars 61-64: the astounding long phrase started by a repeated six-note cell, then resolved with the customary fragments of pentatonic and the descending chromatic passages—on this account also see the introductory repeated notes to "I Got Rhythm."

[1]For an exhaustive discussion on this matter, see "I Got Rhythm" in Dick Hyman's *Professional Chord Changes And Substitutions For 100 Tunes* . . . (Ekay Music); Stefano Zenni: "I Got Rhythm" e il suo lungo "giro" in "Musica Jazz" (Italy), Novembre 1995, pp. 50-52; and Stefano Zenni: Attraverso Gershwin anticiparono il bebop in "Musica Jazz" (Italy), Gennaio 1996, pp. 52-55.

[2]In the statement of the theme (i.e. the first chorus, played by the full ensemble), the chord changes for the A section are:

$$\| \colon \text{Bb} \quad \frac{\text{Bb7}}{\text{D}} \ / \ \text{Eb} \quad \frac{\text{Edim}}{\text{E}} \ / \ \text{Bb} \quad \text{F7} \ / \ \text{Bb} \quad \colon \|$$

[3]In this recording of "Mop Mop," following the guitar solo chorus Tatum played a third piano solo chorus which has not been transcribed here.

[4]This recurrent Tatum figure has been seen in the "Breaks" chapter of this book.

Mop Mop
as recorded by Art Tatum on January 18, 1944

Coleman Hawkins
Transcribed by Riccardo Scivales

The Right Hand According To Tatum

"Rock Me Mama"

On July 13, 1941 Tatum recorded some pieces with a sextet including the blues singer Joe Turner, trumpeter Joe Thomas, guitarist Oscar Moore, bassist Billy Taylor and drummer Yank Porter. Among these pieces, we have transcribed the Tatum solo on "Rock Me Mama," which is a good example of his right hand phrasing on the blues changes. Since in this recording the left hand work is quite sparse and barely audible, the left hand part in this transcription is a simplified adaptation of what is mostly played by guitarist Oscar Moore. Also, the original key of this recording is very probably Gb (we have transcribed it in F for ease in reading and analysis).

In this solo, some of Tatum's distinctive devices are featured, i.e.:

• bar 4: the descending run outlining a decidedly modern (for jazz in 1941) F+7b9. This run seems easier to be played in the original key of Gb:

• bars 5-6: the Fdim7 "broken" arpeggio played on a Bb bass, thus resulting in a Bb7b9 chord (practice transposing this device in all keys);

• bar 8: the little yet delicious variation in the descending F pentatonic run, that is:

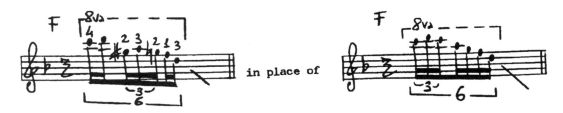

in place of

(Notice that the variation shown above can be applied to all the Tatum descending pentatonic runs);

• bars 10-11: the spectacular run played in irregular seven-note groupings and split between the hands. Also notice that this run is made of descending chromatics and fragments of descending arpeggios; it has a descending-then-ascending contour. These kinds of runs were often used by Tatum and by other major jazz pianists like Earl Hines, and were an integral part of their improvisational language.

As in "Knockin' Myself Out," in "Rock Me Mama" Tatum mixed traditional blues phrasing (see bars 1-4 and 11-12) with his own imaginative and advanced devices, thus creating a new whole that from the harmonic and double-time-phrasing standpoint might likely have been of some inspiration to younger jazzmen of the Forties (on this account, also see the introductory note to "Sweet Georgia Brown").

Rock Me Mama

as recorded by Art Tatum on July 13, 1941

Jones

Transcribed by Riccardo Scivales

"St. Louis Blues"

Tatum's July 26, 1940 solo piano recording of "St. Louis Blues" is one of his most famous interpretations. In the first part, he played some brilliant choruses in boogie-woogie style (he was a master at that, too). The conclusive part—transcribed here—is definitely taken in a Swing style and is a good example of Tatum's approach to the blues when played at medium or fast tempos. Here too, we can appreciate some of his distinctive devices:

• the descending pentatonic runs in bars 4 and 35;

• the very agile, enterprising, and remarkably modern "outside" phrase of bars 8-9;

• the sparkling "Thirds-And-Thumb" run (previously discussed) in bars 19-20;

• another enterprising "outside" phrase in bar 22;

• bar 39 onwards: the bluesy conclusive phrase, using the D Dorian scale on a well-known harmonic pattern for endings. You can practice transposing this phrase in all keys. Here is an example in C:

Throughout this solo, also notice the left hand work, rich in tenths, walking tenth triads, passing chords, two-part devices, and contrapuntal passages. They truly are a perfect example of the Swing Piano technique at its best. In bars 13-18 the accompaniment enhances the Latin quality already found in W.C. Handy's original arrangement of this section of the piece.

St. Louis Blues

as recorded by Art Tatum on July 26, 1940

W.C. Handy

Transcribed by Riccardo Scivales

"Sweet Georgia Brown," #1941:
Art Tatum The Forerunner

"You know this? This is Art Tatum.
More important than Charlie Parker.
People today think Charlie Parker is more important,
but Art Tatum was more important."
...Charles Mingus[1]

According to many musicians' reports, Tatum played his most imaginative, advanced, and experimental things during the "after hours" sessions he loved so much. On those events he very probably felt free of any commercial limitation and was also galvanized by the presence of other jazzmen. Luckily enough, some of the sessions were recorded by Jerry Newman and have been presently reissued on the indispensable "God Is In The House" CD (Onyx 205).

One of the most revealing among these surviving examples of the "after hours" Tatum is the first half of the second chorus of "Sweet Georgia Brown," recorded on September 16, 1941 at the historically famous Clark Monroe's Uptown House in Harlem with Frank Newton (trumpet) and Paul Ebenezer (bass). This chorus—fully transcribed here—was a Tatum solo supported by Paul Ebenezer's string bass. As you can see, in the first part of this chorus (i.e. bars 1-16 of our transcription) Tatum practically does not use the left hand at all, his right hand playing exclusively some daringly advanced "outside" phrases.[2] Also, notice his use of silence, with long rests which are generally not found in his commercial recordings. Considering that this recording was made in 1941, the overall result is definitely astounding, halfway between bebop and Lenni Tristano's works such as "Line Up" and "East Thirty-Second."

Tatum seems indeed to have anticipated some aspects of later jazz styles throughout this episode, which also helps us to better understand Mingus's assertion reported above. Many sources have reported that in 1938 the young Charlie Parker took a three-month job as a dishwasher at Jimmy's Chicken Shack restaurant in Harlem just to have the chance to listen to Tatum, who was playing solo piano there (when Tatum left the job to go to Hollywood, Parker left his own job too). From other sources, we also know that the most important bebop pianist, Bud Powell, idolized Tatum (among other things, he once said: "When I play the ballads, Art Tatum guides my hands").

In the second half of this chorus of "Sweet Georgia Brown" (bar 17 onwards), Tatum turns back to his more customary way of playing. Of particular interest here is the sparkling five-bar long run in triplets and single notes played in bars 25-29 on a I / ii7 / V7 / I (etc.) cadence in F minor. The pattern of this run can be transposed to other keys, too. Also, notice that the melodic fragment played on the F minor chord in bar 25 is repeated on the F minor chord in bar 27, but it is anticipated by an eighth note, thus creating a subtle and quite puzzling shift in the listener's perception:

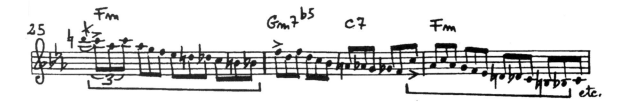

As a closing remark on the long run of bars 25-29, we might add that it seems almost banal when we see it notated down on paper, but it sounds truly fresh and impressive when listened to Tatum's actual recording.

[1]Reported in: Lanieri, Roberto. Io, a lezione da Mingus, in: AA.VV. "Quaderni di Siena Jazz—Charles Mingus," Gennaio-Giugno 1995, p. 109. Laneri reports that Mingus said this while playing "I Can't Get Started" at the piano during one of his lessons at the State University of New York at Buffalo, in the early Seventies.

[2]The chord symbols reported in bars 1-16 of our transcription just show the original chord changes of this song. In this Tatum improvisation we can appreciate his many considerable deviations from them.

The Right Hand According To Tatum

Sweet Georgia Brown

as recorded by Art Tatum on September 16, 1941

Words and Music by Ben Bernie, Maceo Pinkard and Kenneth Casey
Transcribed by Riccardo Scivales

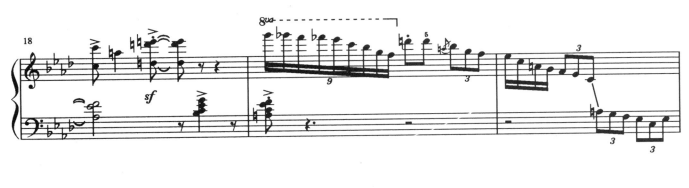

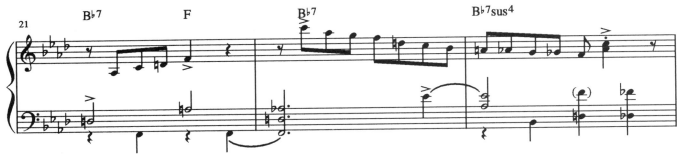

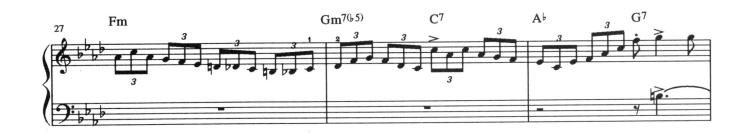

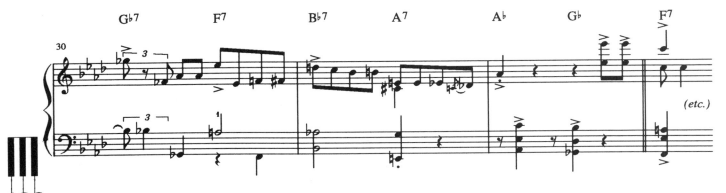

Selected Sources (Music, Books And Articles)

Art Tatum. London: EMI Publishing, 1980.

Calciati, Romolo and Fayenz, Franco. Art Tatum. *Pieve del Cairo* (Italy): Half Note, 1976.

Distler, Jed. *Art Tatum* (6 transcribed solos). New York: Consolidated Music Publishers, 1981.

"Elegy (Excerpt)," Transcribed by Jed Distler. *Keyboard Classics*, November/December 1994, pp. 36-38.

Fayenz, Franco. "Do you remember Art Tatum?" *Jazz* (Italy), Ottobre 1996, pp. 6-13.

"Humoresque," transcribed by Lou Stein. *Jazz & Keyboard Workshop*, Introductory issue, 1986, pp. 2-3.

Hyman, Dick. *Piano Pro*. Katonah, New York: Ekay Music, 1992 (also includes "Thinking About Art Tatum," "The Art Tatum Tribute At Town Hall," and "Art Tatum In Slow Motion" chapters, plus the "Onyx Mood" piano solo in Tatum's style).

Jazz, Blues, Boogie And Swing For Piano, Edited by Ronnie S. Schiff. Melville, New York: MCA/Mills, 1977 (also includes Tatum's "Carnegie Hall Bounce" and "Gang O'Nothin").

Jazz Piano 2, transcribed by Brian Prestley. Woodford Green, Essex (England): International Music Publications, 1986 (also includes Tatum's interpretation of "I Got Rhythm").

Jazz Piano 4, transcribed by Brian Prestley. Woodford Green, Essex (England): International Music Publications, 1986 (also includes Tatum's interpretation of "Body and Soul").

Lester, James, *Too Marvelous for Words—The Life & Genius of Art Tatum*. Oxford University Press, 1994 (this accurate biography also includes a rich bibliography).

Mayer, Steven. "Tatum & Liszt At The Keyboard." *Keyboard Classics*, March/April 1990, pp. 12-17 (also included is the transcription of Tatum's recording of "I Know That You Know").

Morgenstern, Dan. Liner notes to the "Art Tatum God Is In The House" CD (Onyx 205).

Piras, Marcello. "L'uomo che offrì un fossile ai suoi amici." *Musica Jazz* (Italy), Febbraio 1995, pp. 56-59.

Schuller, Gunther. *The Swing Era.* Oxford University Press, 1989.

Spencer, Ray. Liner notes to *Art Tatum—The V-Discs CD* (Black Lion BLCD760114).

Stein, Lou. "Transcription And Analysis Of A Tatum Solo." *Jazz & Keyboard Workshop*, Introductory issue, 1986, pp. 1 and 4-5.

Taylor, Billy. *Jazz Piano—A Jazz History.* Dubuque, Iowa: Wm. C. Brown Company Publishers, 1982.

"Tatum Meets Horowitz—An Interview With Steven Mayer." *Keyboard Classics*, November/December 1994, pp. 34-35 (also included is Peter Coughlin's review of the *Steven Mayer Plays Art Tatum* CD).

The Art Tatum Collection, Transcribed by Brent Edstrom (15 solos). Milwaukee: Hal Leonard, 1996.

"Wrap Your Troubles in Dreams," as played by Art Tatum. *The Piano Stylist & Jazz Workshop*, October-November 1990, pp. 1-3.

About the Author

Riccardo Scivales was born in Venezia, Italy, where he continues to live. He studied piano privately and graduated from the University of Venezia in 1986 with a degree in Music History. As a pianist and composer, he has worked for various stage productions and led the Quanah Parker and Tumbadoras music groups. He played at Gran Caffé Chioggia in Venezia's St. Mark's Square for many years. At present he performs with his own Mi Ritmo quintet specializing in Latin music.

He is the author of *Harlem Stride Piano Solos* and *Learn To Play Latin Piano*, both published by Ekay Music. His other books, *Famous Italian Songs*, *Famous Italian Opera Arias*, *Echoes of Venice* (piano arrangements), and *Dick Wellstood—Jazz Piano Solos* (transcribed solos) are published by the Neil A. Kjos Music Company (San Diego, California). He has written hundreds of radio programs on jazz for RAI-Radiotelevisione Italiana. Many of his essays, piano arrangements and transcriptions have been published in various books and music magazines—such as *The Piano Stylist*, *Keyboard Classics*, *Piano Today*, *Blu Jazz*, *Jazz*, and *Musica Jazz*—in Italy and the United States.